Territorial Claims in the
Sino-Soviet Conflict

Documents & Analysis

Dennis J. Doolin

Hoover Institution Studies: 7

Territorial Claims in the Sino-Soviet Conflict

Hoover Institution Studies: 7

Territorial Claims in the
Sino-Soviet Conflict
Documents & Analysis

Dennis J. Doolin

*The Hoover Institution
on War, Revolution, and Peace
Stanford University, 1965*

The Hoover Institution on War, Revolution, and Peace, founded at Stanford University in 1919 by Herbert Hoover, is a center for advanced study and research on public and international affairs in the twentieth century. The views expressed in its publications are entirely those of the authors and do not necessarily reflect the views of the Hoover Institution.

FOREWORD

In spite of the growing evidence of a falling out between the leaders of Communist China and the Soviet Union which has been accumulating over the past several years, it was not until early 1964 that either side openly brought out one of the key issues in the rift—China's demand for the restitution by the Soviet Union of almost 600,000 square miles of land, "grabbed" by Imperial Russia at a time when China was unable to oppose this.

The issue itself had been clear enough for decades. When the Chinese Communists "liberated" mainland China in 1949, they acquired the title to claims and grievances dating back to the middle years of the Ch'ing Dynasty. At the end of the eighteenth century, an expanding Russia began a gradual process of encroachment on the vast territories of Siberia which culminated in the establishment of Vladivostok as a Pacific port. At least a portion of the territory acquired by Russia in this period of expansion belonged—for longer or shorter periods—to the Chinese Empire and was ceded to Russia in the "unequal" treaties of the nineteenth century. As China emerges from the lethargy of past centuries, its claims for the restitution of these areas are backed by its growing power.

In Chinese eyes, Russian encroachment on Chinese territorial sovereignty continued long after the period of "imperialist expansion" on the part of other European states had come to a close. The most notable example was the detachment of Outer Mongolia from Chinese control and its establishment as a "People's Republic" in 1924. Also serving as a constant irritant was a long succession of border "incidents" in Chinese Turkestan, particularly in the Ili area. Under both the Czars and the Commissars, the Russians have been poor neighbors at best. The catalog of complaints has grown tediously long.

The Communist victory in China and its entry into the world Communist system brought a temporary halt to the public expression of disagreements on territorial questions. But even in this new relationship, the Chinese provided evidence that territorial matters had not been forgotten by publishing occasional maps showing disputed areas as belonging historically to China. Such gambits elicited no response from the Soviets during the era of outwardly tranquil relations, although they did not pass without notice in Russia or elsewhere.

In spite of such evidence of subsurface dissension and the occasional reports of actual clashes between Chinese and Soviet forces on the northwestern borders of Turkestan, the Communist Party leaders, both Chinese and Russian, maintained a dignified silence. In the summer of 1964, however, the pressures became too great to prevent this issue from being included in the polemics within the Communist world.

Mr. Doolin's brief sketch of the background and recent course of events which have a bearing on this significant aspect of Sino-Russian relations is accompanied by the texts of many of the key documents involved, including ex-Premier Khrushchev's policy statement on colonialism of December 12, 1962. Other pre-1964 materials provide clues to the attitudes and convictions underlying the open break on the territorial issue which did not come until July 1964.

This study does not attempt to interpret the territorial issue as a factor in the Sino-Soviet split, although it has undoubtedly played a key part. Both the seriousness of the rift and the importance of the dispute over Russian territorial acquisitions are questions which will require a longer historical perspective to decide. The essential purpose here is to provide an objective presentation of the basic facts in the case, supported by careful translations of official statements, press releases, and monitored broadcasts from Russian, Chinese, and Japanese sources. Much of this material has failed to attract the attention it deserves, and some is appearing here for the first time in English. The original documents form part of the collections at the Hoover Institution and are available for inspection by any interested student.

WITOLD S. SWORAKOWSKI
Assistant Director,
Hoover Institution

February 10, 1965

ACKNOWLEDGMENT

For their expert advice and assistance, I wish to express my thanks to Professor Witold S. Sworakowski, Assistant Director of the Hoover Institution on War, Revolution, and Peace, Professor Yuan-li Wu of the University of San Francisco, and Mr. J. G. Bell of the Stanford University Press. Any errors of omission or commission are, however, mine alone.

DENNIS J. DOOLIN

Hoover Institution
January 10, 1965

CONTENTS

TERRITORIAL CLAIMS IN THE SINO-SOVIET CONFLICT

MAP 1: Soviet Asia, Central Asia, East Asia, and periphery.

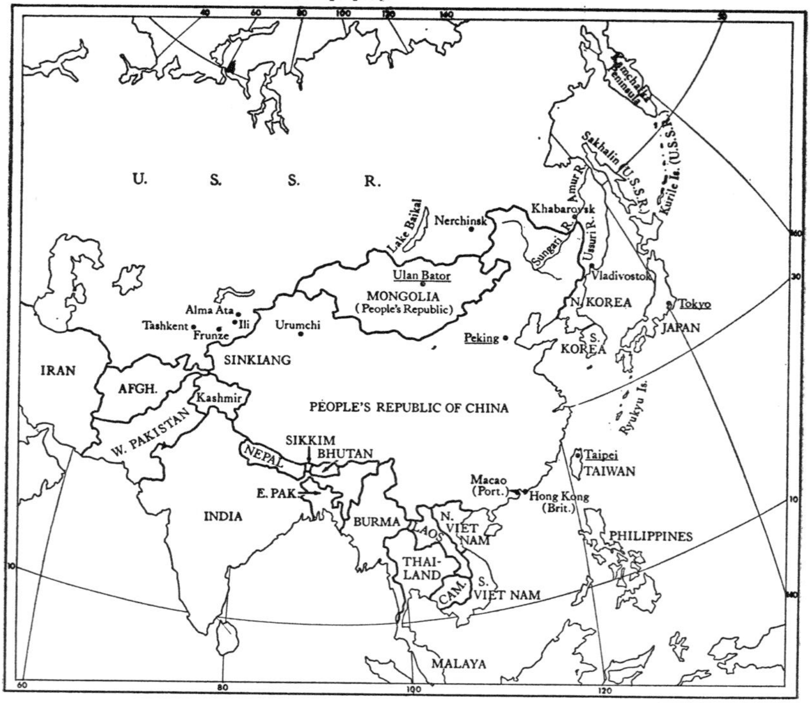

INTRODUCTION

This book consists of documents on the territorial dispute between the Soviet Union and Communist China which came into the open early in 1963 and ultimately led to a number of bitter exchanges between the two countries. It is not suggested that the territorial question is the central issue in the Sino-Soviet conflict. The aim is simply to document a little-known side of Sino-Soviet relations.

HISTORICAL BACKGROUND

The first clash between Russian and Chinese troops took place in the valley of the Amur River in the 1680's. Sporadic fighting continued until 1689, when a treaty between the two countries (the first between China and a European state) was signed at Nerchinsk. Among other things, the Treaty of Nerchinsk delimited the frontier, recognizing that China owned much of the land north of the Amur River, and stated that no Russian vessels could travel along the waterway. It also recognized Khalka (Eastern) Mongolia and the Kalmuk district of northern Sinkiang (Chinese Turkestan) as within China's sphere of influence.[1] (See Map 1.)

The Treaty of Nerchinsk ostensibly remained in force until the middle of the nineteenth century. This was a time of great trouble for China, notably the Opium War with Britain (1839–1842), the Taiping Rebellion (1850–1864), and the continuing pressure by the Great Powers for territorial and other concessions. The Russians took advantage of the situation to send colonists and troops down the Amur; and in 1858, negotiating from this position of strength, they forced the Treaty of Aigun on the hapless Ch'ing (Manchu) Government. Under the terms of this treaty, China ceded to Russia all ter-

---

[1] Kenneth Scott Latourette, *The Chinese: Their History and Culture,* 3rd rev. ed. (New York: Macmillan, 1959), pp. 317, 353. A readable, more detailed account is to be found in James Vivian Davidson-Huston, *Russia and China: From the Huns to Mao Tse-tung* (London: R. Hale, 1960), pp. 72–109 *passim.*

ritory north of the Amur River (in effect already occupied by the Cossacks) and agreed that the area east of the Ussuri River would be under a condominium of the two empires.

Although the Ch'ing Government in the end refused to ratify the Treaty of Aigun, the essential provisions were confirmed by the Treaty of Peking in 1860, except that in the new treaty the area east of the Ussuri was ceded outright to Russia. Furthermore, the so-called Kazakh "picket line" was to be the frontier of Sinkiang in the northwest, thereby giving Russia a large portion of the Ili region of Chinese Turkestan. It was by this treaty that Russia expanded to the shores of the Pacific Ocean.

Following the overthrow of the Ch'ing Dynasty and the establishment of the Republic of China in 1911, Chinese nationalists were quick to demand the abrogation of all unequal treaties, together with the restoration of China's "traditional" frontiers. As a result, a Russo-Chinese protocol was signed in 1912 which stipulated that Outer Mongolia, although it would enjoy internal autonomy, was indeed a part of China proper. Moreover, after the establishment of the Soviet regime in 1917, Russia's Acting Commissar for Foreign Affairs, L. M. Karakhan, issued his famous Declaration of July 25, 1919, repudiating all unequal treaties concluded between the Czarist Government and China, as well as any and all privileges enjoyed by Russia in China, Mongolia, and Manchuria.[2] Soviet representatives stated later that the Karakhan Declaration was merely a fundamental program to be used as a basis for negotiation, and not a precise list of concrete steps to be taken by the Soviet Government. However, Chinese nationalists took the Declaration in the latter sense, and the 1924 Agreement on General Principles (under which Soviet Russia surrendered extraterritoriality and reaffirmed its recognition of Chinese sovereignty over Outer Mongolia) served only to strengthen that feeling.

[2] For the text of the Karakhan Declaration, see Allen S. Whiting, *Soviet Policies in China, 1917–1924* (New York: Columbia University Press, 1954), pp. 269–71. Also see the Karakhan Manifesto (September 27, 1920): "The Government of the Russian Socialist Federated Soviet Republics declares as void all the treaties concluded by the former Government of Russia with China, renounces all the annexations of Chinese territory, all the concessions in China, and returns to China free of charge, and forever, all that was ravenously taken from her by the Tsar's Government and by the Russian bourgeoisie." *Ibid.*, pp. 272–75, quotation from p. 273.

In the current Sino-Soviet territorial dispute, Soviet spokesmen have made much of a Chinese Communist map, published in 1954, which shows large areas of the Soviet Union as "rightfully" belonging to China (reproduced here as Map 2). Actually, this was nothing new. During the Republican period (1911–1949), Chinese maps made similar—and in some cases more sweeping—claims (see Map 3). Sun Yat-sen decried China's loss of Taiwan, the Pescadores, Burma, Annam, the Amur and Ussuri river basins, and the areas north of the Ili, Khokand, and Amur rivers, as well as such tributary areas as the Ryukyus, Thailand, Borneo, the Sulu Archipelago, Java, Ceylon, Nepal, and Bhutan.[3] In a similar vein, Chiang Kai-shek wrote: "Indeed, after having witnessed the tragedy of the loss of the Liuchiu [Ryukyu] Islands, Hong Kong, Formosa, the Pescadores, Annam, Burma, and Korea, China was confronted with the great danger of imminent partition of her territory."[4] And, although Outer Mongolia had gained its "independence" in the early 1920's, Mao Tse-tung in 1936 spoke of its automatically becoming a part of the Chinese state after the Communist victory.[5] Thus, the present conflict in many ways contains little more than variations on an old, old theme.

THE CURRENT CONTROVERSY

After the Communist victory on the Chinese mainland in 1949, the territorial question apparently was not raised. The Sino-Soviet Treaty of Friendship, Alliance, and Mutual Assistance, concluded in February of 1950, somewhat resembled the unequal treaties of earlier times (joint Sino-Soviet stock companies, joint control of key railroads, and Soviet naval bases in Port Arthur–Dairen), but there were no overt protests from Peking at that time. Mao Tse-tung attempted to discuss the status of Outer Mongolia with Khrushchev and Bulganin in 1954. However, in the Chairman's words, "they refused to talk to us" (Doc. 14). Chou En-lai also was unsuccessful in discussions with Khrushchev in January 1957 on a wider range of territorial

[3] Sun Yat-sen, *San Min Chu I* (Shanghai: Commercial Press, 1929), pp. 33–35.

[4] Chiang Kai-shek, *China's Destiny* (New York: Macmillan, 1947), p. 242; also the unauthorized translation, with notes, by Philip Jaffe (New York: Roy Publishers, 1947), p. 58.

[5] As quoted in Edgar Snow, *Red Star Over China* (New York: Modern Library, 1944), p. 96.

MAP 2: "The Old Democratic Revolutionary Era (1840-1919) — Chinese Territories Taken by Imperialism." From Liu P'ei-hua, ed., *Chung-kuo chin-tai chien-shih,* (A Short History of Modern China), (Peking: I ch'ang shu chü, 1954), following p. 253. Key numbers added for the present book.

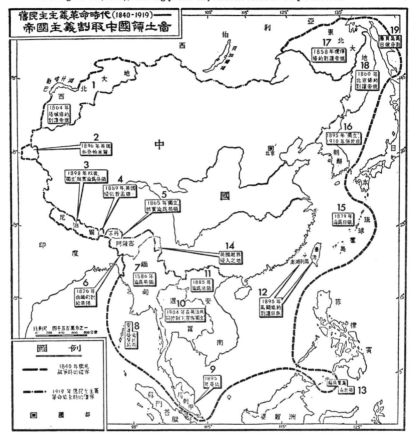

KEY TO MAP 2

(Translation of the information given in boxes on the map.)

1. The Great Northwest: seized by Imperial Russia under the Treaty of Chuguchak, 1864. [Parts of present Soviet Kazakhstan, Kirghizstan, and Tadzhikstan.]
2. Pamirs: secretly divided between England and Russia in 1896.
3. Nepal: went to England after "independence" in 1898.
4. Sikkim: occupied by England in 1889.
5. Bhutan: went to England after "independence" in 1865.
6. Assam: given to England by Burma in 1826.
7. Burma: became part of the British Empire in 1886.
8. Andaman Archipelago: went to England.
9. Malaya: occupied by England in 1895.
10. Thailand: declared "independent" under joint Anglo-French control in 1904.
11. Annam: occupied by France in 1885. [Covers present North Vietnam, South Vietnam, Laos, and Cambodia.]
12. Taiwan and P'eng-hu Archipelago [Pescadores]: relinquished to Japan per the Treaty of Shimonoseki, 1895.
13. Sulu Archipelago: went to England.
14. Region where the British crossed the border and committed aggression.
15. Ryukyu Archipelago: occupied by Japan in 1879.
16. Korea: "independent" in 1895—annexed by Japan in 1910.
17. The Great Northeast: seized by Imperial Russia under the Treaty of Aigun, 1858.
18. The Great Northeast: seized by Imperial Russia under the Treaty of Peking, 1860.
19. Sakhalin: divided between Russia and Japan.

MAP 3: Taken from Hsieh Pin, *Chung-kuo sang-ti shih*, (A History of China's Lost Territory), (Shanghai: Hsin-hua shu chü, 1925).

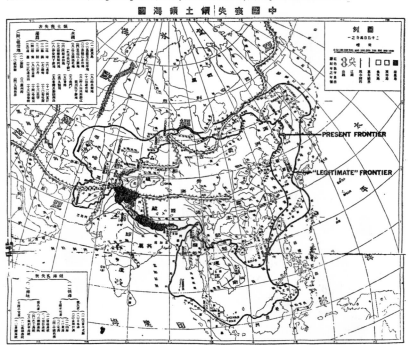

issues. However, Chou stated in July of 1964 that "the issue was kept secret because the Sino-Soviet dispute was not public at that time" (Doc. 16).

Later in 1957, during the Hundred Flowers period, several prominent Chinese professed to see little difference between Czarist and Soviet imperialism,[6] but the Chinese Communist Party was quick to silence such talk. Little was heard of any territorial dispute, actual or potential, until the first quarter of 1963.

It would appear that, although the undercurrent has always been there, the *overt* controversy over the Sino-Soviet border was actually an unforeseen by-product of the Cuban missile crisis of October 1962. The Chinese criticized the Soviets on two points: stationing the missiles in Cuba in the first place ("adventurism") and removing the missiles to avert a possible nuclear collision with the United States ("capitulationism").

Khrushchev addressed himself to these charges in a report to the Supreme Soviet on December 12, 1962. In effect, this report (Doc. 1) was an argument for pragmatic action rather than action dictated by ideological absolutes. China, after all, had not "liberated" Hong Kong and Macao; this was not "capitulationism" on China's part, but rather simple common sense. So had it been with Cuba.

Shortly thereafter, the Communist Party of the United States (CPUSA), in an open letter to the Chinese Communist Party (CCP), also took issue with the Chinese position on the Cuban crisis (Doc. 2): "Our Chinese comrades . . . are even today, correctly, not following the adventurous policy in Taiwan, Hong Kong, and Macao that they advocate for others. Why this double-standard approach?"

The Chinese Communist leaders reacted sharply to these counter-arguments and replied to the statement of the CPUSA in early March 1963 (Doc. 3). At this time, the Chinese brought up the subject of the old unequal treaties and listed nine of them, three of which were concluded between China and Czarist Russia and still remained in force, the Karakhan Declaration notwithstanding. The Chinese statement concluded on a somewhat ominous note: "In raising questions of this kind, do you intend to raise all the questions of unequal treaties

[6] Notably Huang Ch'i-hsiang, former Nationalist general and member of the National Defense Council of the Communist regime, as quoted in "Huang Ch'i-hsiang Unmasked as a Two-faced, Anti-Communist, and Anti-Socialist Monster," *New China News Agency*, Peking, July 29, 1957.

and have a general settlement? Has it ever entered your heads what the consequences will be? Can you seriously believe that this will do you any good?" This warning was obviously directed at Khrushchev rather than the CPUSA, for the Chinese stated that they knew both the source of this charge and "the purpose of the person who manufactured it."

Aside from scattered reports of incidents in the northwest sector of the Sino-Soviet border (Docs. 4 and 5), little additional public comment on the matter was made by either side until the end of 1963. At that time, Premier Khrushchev sent a message to the heads of state of all countries proposing an international treaty on the renunciation of the use of force in resolving territorial disputes or frontier questions (Doc. 6). The Chinese Communist press did not report Khrushchev's proposal, except to say that the Soviet Union had recently given further evidence of its intention to seek solidarity with the West.

In February, the Yugoslav news agency Tanjug announced that a Soviet delegation had arrived in Peking to discuss the border problem (Doc. 8). However, it soon became apparent that little progress was being made in these talks. Six days after the arrival of the frontier experts, the Central Committee of the CCP addressed a letter to its Soviet counterpart complaining of "frequent breaches of the *status quo* on the border," occupation of Chinese territory, and "large-scale subversive activities in Chinese frontier areas" (Doc. 9). Furthermore, the Chinese letter placed the Soviet leaders in the same category as the "reactionary nationalists of India who have deliberately created border disputes with China."

During the next three months, Soviet spokesmen countered with protests against Chinese border provocations (Doc. 10) and refutations of Chinese frontier claims (Doc. 11).[7] In addition, the Soviet news media accused the Chinese of collaborating with British and American capitalist interests in Hong Kong, the result being that the three states were "jointly exploiting the working people" (Doc. 13). In July of 1964, the Chinese Communists announced the signing

[7] They also scored Chinese Communist praise of Genghis Khan as a "historically progressive" person—an understandable criticism, inasmuch as the Golden Horde of Genghis Khan, "founder" of the Yüan (Mongol) Dynasty (1279–1368), had advanced into Europe proper and established tyrannical Khanates in South Russia and Persia that survived for over a century. (See the remarks by academician Roman Samarin, Tass International Service, Moscow, April 11, 1964.)

of a border protocol with Outer Mongolia. As with the Sino-Mongolian Boundary Treaty of December 1962, few details were given.[8] These agreements ostensibly delimited the Sino-Mongolian frontier, but since all Chinese advisers and technicians were soon afterwards ordered by the Outer Mongolian Government to leave the country, it would appear that the Sino-Mongolian border issue is far from settled.

The next development—the most striking of the sequence and one of the most interesting public events in the Sino-Soviet conflict to date—involved Mao Tse-tung himself. On July 10, in an interview with the leader of a Japanese Socialist Party mission to Peking (Doc. 14), Mao criticized the Soviet Union for its "territorial ambitions" both in Asia and in Europe, stated that the CCP was prepared to continue to "wage this war [against the Communist Party of the Soviet Union] for another twenty-five years," and explicitly supported the Japanese Socialists' demand that the USSR return the Kurile Islands to Japan. He concluded: "About a hundred years ago, the area to the east of [Lake] Baikal became Russian territory, and since then Vladivostok, Khabarovsk, Kamchatka, and other areas have been Soviet territory. We have not yet presented our account for this list." Although the Chinese Communist press did not carry the interview, Japanese newspapers gave it extensive coverage, along with a statement by Premier Chou En-lai supporting Mao's position (Docs. 15 and 16), and adding that secret talks had been held on the territorial question in January of 1957.

Mao's position regarding the Kuriles may well have reflected his fear of a possible Russo-Japanese accord, which, given Communist China's embattled relations with the USSR and India, would leave the Chinese with no hope of a major Asian ally in any campaign against Taiwan. In any event, Mao's statement about the Kuriles was apparently secondary in his own mind to his attack on Soviet expansionism in Europe—specifically, in Rumania, Germany, Poland, and Finland. "The Russians," Mao said, "took everything they could."[9] Curiously enough, the only European support for Mao's

[8] For a report on the 1962 agreement, see *Peking Review,* No. 52, December 28, 1962; text of treaty in Peking *Jen-min jih-pao* (People's Daily), March 26, 1963.

[9] It is interesting to note that, in decrying the Soviet Union's illegal possession of territory in Europe, Mao was actually criticizing Stalin, for these areas were incorporated into the USSR during his rule.

statement came not from Eastern Europe, but from a rightist and militantly anti-Communist Munich newspaper, *Deutsche National Zeitung und Soldaten Zeitung,* which on August 21 published a map displaying both the Chinese and the German territorial claims against the Soviet Union.[10]

On September 2, *Pravda* examined Mao's views in a lengthy editorial (Doc. 19). Mao's statements in regard to the "unfair distribution of territory" were condemned as nothing less than a new version of the *Lebensraum* theory; the Chinese Communist leader was portrayed as a latter-day follower of Hitler, Tojo, and others who had advocated "an openly expansionist program with far-reaching pretensions." Further, Soviet spokesmen continued to criticize the Chinese for the 1954 map (pp. 16–17). Although Peking had repudiated this map in 1963, the Chinese Communists reportedly distributed a booklet at a 1964 trade fair in Mexico City containing a map that continued to show the Soviet Maritime Provinces as part of China.[11]

On September 15, Premier Khrushchev had a lengthy talk with members of a Japanese parliamentary delegation (Doc. 26), in which he clearly indicated that the USSR had no intention of returning the Kurile Islands to Japan and deplored expansionism in carefully chosen words: "Given up-to-date weapons of annihilation, it is now particularly dangerous and . . . criminal to search for wealth through the extension of 'Lebensraum.' "

Khrushchev also renewed his proposal for an international agreement outlawing the use of force in the solution of territorial problems. This was followed up by a letter from Soviet Foreign Minister Andrei Gromyko to U Thant, Secretary-General of the United Nations, requesting that a Soviet resolution, "On the Renunciation by States of the Use of Force for Settling Territorial and Frontier Disputes," be included on the agenda of the Nineteenth Session of the General Assembly (Doc. 27).

Finally, the Soviet Premier reminded his Japanese visitors that, if the Russian Czars had been expansionists, so had the Chinese Emperors who seized Mongolia, Tibet, and Sinkiang. Elaborating on this, he noted: "Let us take Sinkiang, for example. Have the Chinese

[10] *Deutsche National Zeitung und Soldaten Zeitung,* August 21, 1964, p. 1; also see Doc. 26.

[11] "Quarterly Chronicle and Documentation," *China Quarterly,* No. 18, April–June 1964, p. 241.

been living there from time immemorial? The Sinkiang indigenous population differs sharply from the Chinese ethnically, linguistically, and in other respects. They are Uighur, Kazakh, Kirghiz, and other peoples. Chinese Emperors conquered them in the past and deprived them of their independence."

The Chinese Communists were infuriated by this statement. In his talk with the Japanese Socialists, Mao had noted that "the Soviet Union is concentrating troops along its borders"; now Khrushchev was claiming that Sinkiang does not belong to China. On October 1, in one of the fiercest statements in the Sino-Soviet conflict to date, Saifudin, alternate member of the Central Committee of the CCP and Chairman of the Sinkiang Uighur Autonomous Region, answered Khrushchev (Doc. 29): "If the Khrushchev revisionists dare to stretch out their evil hands to invade and occupy our territory, they will certainly be repulsed. . . . Their evil hands will be cut off as relentlessly as were those of the Indian reactionaries when they invaded China."[12]

CONCLUSION

With the ouster of Premier Khrushchev in October of 1964, the open polemics ceased for a time, possibly because the Chinese had hoped for better things from Brezhnev and Kosygin. And it is a fact that the Chinese were quick to list the territorial dispute as one of the key events that led to Khrushchev's dismissal. The theoretical journal of the Central Committee of the CCP, *Hung-ch'i*, stated: "He engineered border disputes between China and the Soviet Union and even conducted large-scale subversive activities in Sinkiang. He backed the reactionaries in India in their armed attacks on socialist China and, together with the United States, incited and helped them to perpetrate armed provocations against China by giving them military aid."[13]

However, there is apparently little reason other than Chinese wishful thinking to assume that Khrushchev's successors will be any better

[12] In the same vein, the resolution adopted by the second session of the Third People's Congress of the Sinkiang Uighur Autonomous Region stated that Sinkiang was an "inseparable part of China" and that "any attempts to undermine the great unity of the nationalities in China or to occupy Sinkiang by force are doomed to failure." *New China News Agency*, Urumchi, November 5, 1964.

[13] Editorial, "Why Khrushchev Fell," *Hung-ch'i* (Red Flag), No. 21–22, November 21, 1964; *Peking Review*, No. 48, November 27, 1964, p. 7.

disposed toward China than Khrushchev himself. Aside from him, the divisive elements that gave rise to the Sino-Soviet conflict are still present. Communist China continues to be frustrated in its attempts to "liberate" Taiwan; the Soviet Union refrains from moves that might bring about a confrontation with the United States similar to that of October 1962; and the Brezhnev-Kosygin leadership has announced that "peaceful coexistence" remains a cornerstone of Soviet policy— in effect, Khrushchevism without Khrushchev. Thus, the Sino-Soviet conflict continues, and territorial problems remain important.[14] One suspects that they will not be easily resolved, no matter who rules in Moscow or Peking.

[14] The November issue of the journal *Problems of Peace and Socialism,* published by *Pravda* and edited by a member of the Central Committee of the CPSU, contained many articles criticizing Chinese Communist policy (Doc. 30). The issue went on sale on November 14, the same day that Chou En-lai returned to Peking from a series of talks in Moscow with the new Soviet leaders.

DOCUMENTS

1

KHRUSHCHEV TO THE SUPREME SOVIET

(Excerpts from a speech by Premier Khrushchev at an evening meeting of the Supreme Soviet, December 12, 1962; Moscow Domestic Service broadcast, December 12, 1962. A partial text was printed in the *New York Times*, Western Edition, December 13, 1962, p. 2.)

Comrade deputies, one must say that strident, dissatisfied voices against the peaceful solution of the Cuban [missile] crisis were also raised from another quarter. They came from people who call themselves Marxist-Leninists, although in actual fact they have nothing in common with Marxist-Leninists.

. . .

One must be very careful and not hastily indulge in irresponsible accusations that some are implementing an orthodox policy while others are pursuing an erroneous policy or that some are carrying on an offensive against imperialism while others are allegedly displaying tolerance [toward imperialism]. These problems can be correctly understood, and these and other actions properly evaluated, only if one takes account of the time, place, and circumstances in which one has to act. Thus, India has achieved the liberation of Goa, Diu, and Damão. These were the remnants of colonialism on Indian soil. Even when the British colonizers were thrown out of India, Portugal kept its colonies there which spread the stink of colonialism. India and the Indian Government showed patience for several years, suffered this, and then threw out the colonialists in one fell swoop. Did they act correctly? Of course.

. . .

When Indonesia gained its freedom, the Dutch colonialists tried to keep West Irian. However, the Indonesian people and their government forced the colonialists to leave West Irian. We rendered what help we could to Indonesia in its struggle; we welcome the liberation of West Irian and its reunion with independent Indonesia.

On the China coast, at the mouth of the Hsi River, lies Macao. This is a very small territory which one can hardly spot on the map.

The Portuguese leased it in the sixteenth century; in 1887, they tore it away from China and turned it into a colony.

There also exists a British colony—Hong Kong. It is situated in the Hsi River Delta, literally within a stone's throw of the important city of Canton. From these colonies rises a smell that is no better than the stench that rose from colonial Goa.

But does anyone accuse China because remnants of colonialism remain untouched on her territory? It would be incorrect to prod China into taking actions that she regards as premature. If the Government of the People's Republic of China endures [the continued existence of] Macao and Hong Kong, then there must obviously be good reasons for this. Therefore, it would be stupid to heap accusations on their heads that this supposedly represents concessions to the British and Portuguese colonialists, that it is an act of appeasement on their part.

Or perhaps it is a retreat from Marxism-Leninism on their part? Nothing of the kind. This simply means that the Government of the People's Republic of China is taking into account the actual situation and assessing realistically its possibilities of action. . . .

We are not hurrying them—on the contrary, we say: settle this in accordance with the interests of your own country and the interests of the whole socialist camp.

And what would have happened if, during the Cuban crisis, we had not shown the necessary restraint and had listened to the urgings of the ultrarevolutionary loudmouths? We would have sunk into the morass of a new world war, a thermonuclear war!

2

THE CPUSA REPROACHES THE CCP

(Excerpts from "The Cuba Crisis and the Struggle for World Peace," *The Worker*, New York, January 13, 1963; reprint of CPUSA statement of January 9, 1963.)

The Communist Party of the U.S. regretfully finds it necessary to take sharp public issue with the policy of the Chinese Communist Party in respect to the Caribbean [i.e., Cuban missile] crisis and in respect to its wrong position on peaceful coexistence in general.

. . .

One could say at this point that our Chinese comrades, who set an example of flexibility in their heroic struggle for liberation, are even today, correctly, not following the adventurous policy in Taiwan, Hong Kong, and Macao that they advocate for others. Why this double-standard approach?

. . .

As regards the unfortunate Chinese-Indian border conflict, we have already made clear our position, and have from the first day called for an end to the fighting and for the solution of this question by peaceful negotiation. But irrespective of the merits in the dispute, and recognizing the merits of the Chinese position, and precisely because of the danger from imperialism and its collaborators within India, the fact is that China was embroiled in the unfortunate conflict at the very moment when imperialism threatened the peace of the entire world.

3

THE CCP'S REPLY TO THE CPUSA

(Excerpts from "A Comment on the Statement of the Communist Party of the U.S.A.," an editorial in *Jen-min jih-pao,* Peking, March 8, 1963.)

On January 9 of this year, the Communist Party of the United States of America issued a statement publicly attacking the Communist Party of China. Certain comrades of the CPUSA have also made . . . other attacks on the Chinese Communist Party in recent months.

. . .

With an ulterior purpose, the statement of the CPUSA referred to Taiwan, Hong Kong, and Macao. It said that the Chinese comrades were "correctly, not following the adventurous policy in Taiwan, Hong Kong, and Macao that they advocate for others. Why this double-standard approach?"

We know from what quarter they have learned this ridiculous charge. And we know, too, the purpose of the person [i.e., Khrushchev] who manufactured it.

Here we should like to answer all those who have raised this matter. For us, there has never been a question of a "double standard." We have only one standard, whether in dealing with the question of Taiwan, whether in dealing with the questions of Hong Kong and Macao, or whether in dealing with all international questions, and that standard is Marxism-Leninism, proletarian internationalism, the interests of the Chinese people and of the people of the world, the interests of world peace, and the revolutionary cause of the people of all countries. In international struggles, we are opposed both to adventurism and to capitulationism. These two hats can never fit our heads.

Inasmuch as some persons have mentioned Taiwan, Hong Kong, and Macao, we are obliged to discuss a little of the history of imperialist aggression against China.

In the hundred years or so prior to the victory of the Chinese revolution, the imperialist and colonial powers—the United States, Britain, France, Czarist Russia, Germany, Japan, Italy, Austria, Belgium, the Netherlands, Spain, and Portugal—carried out unbridled aggression against China. They compelled the governments of old China to sign a large number of unequal treaties—the Treaty of Nanking of 1842, the Treaty of Aigun of 1858, the Treaty of Tientsin of 1858, the Treaty of Peking of 1860, the Treaty of Ili of 1881, the Protocol of Lisbon of 1887, the Treaty of Shimonoseki of 1895, the Convention for the Extension of Hong Kong of 1898, the International Protocol of 1901, etc. By virtue of these unequal treaties, they annexed Chinese territory in the north, south, east, and west and held leased territories on the seaboard and in the hinterland of China. Some seized Taiwan and the P'eng-hu Archipelago [Pescadores Islands], some occupied Hong Kong and forcibly leased Kowloon, some put Macao under perpetual occupation, and so forth.

At the time the People's Republic of China was inaugurated, our Government declared that it would examine the treaties concluded by previous Chinese governments with foreign governments, treaties that had been left over by history, and would recognize, abrogate, revise, or renegotiate them according to their respective contents. In this respect, our policy toward the socialist countries is fundamentally different from our policy toward the imperialist countries. When we deal with various imperialist countries, we take differing circumstances into consideration and make distinctions in our policy. As a matter of fact, many of these treaties have been abrogated or have been replaced by new ones. With regard to the outstanding issues, which are a legacy from the past, we have always held that, when conditions are ripe, they should be settled peacefully through negotiations and that, pending a settlement, the *status quo* should be maintained. Within this category are the questions of Hong Kong, Kowloon, and Macao and the questions of all those boundaries which have not been formally delimited in each case by the parties concerned. As for Taiwan and the P'eng-hu Archipelago, they were restored to China in 1945, and the question now is the U.S. imperialist invasion and occupation of them and U.S. imperialist interference in China's internal affairs. We Chinese people are determined to exercise our sovereign right to liberate our territory of Taiwan; at the same time, through the ambassadorial talks between China and the United States in Warsaw, we are striving to solve the question of effecting the withdrawal of U.S. armed forces from Taiwan and the Taiwan Strait. Our position as described above accords not only with the interests of the Chinese people but also with the interests of the people of the socialist camp and the people of the whole world.

Why is it that after the Caribbean crisis, this correct policy of ours suddenly became a topic of discussion among certain persons and a theme for their anti-China campaign?

These heroes are apparently very pleased with themselves for having picked up a stone from a cesspool, with which they believe they can instantly fell the Chinese. But whom has this filthy stone actually hit?

You are not unaware that such questions as those of Hong Kong and Macao relate to the category of unequal treaties left over by history, treaties which the imperialists imposed on China. It may be asked: In raising questions of this kind, do you intend to raise all the questions of unequal treaties and have a general settlement? Has it ever entered your heads what the consequences will be? Can you seriously believe that this will do you any good?

4

SUBVERSION IN SINKIANG

(Excerpt from a joint statement by the Editorial Departments of *Jen-min jih-pao* and *Hung-ch'i*, "The Origin and Development of the Differences between the Leaders of the CPSU and Ourselves," September 6, 1963; reprinted in *Peking Review*, No. 37, September 13, 1963, pp. 6–23.)

In April and May 1962, the leaders of the CPSU [Communist Party of the Soviet Union] used their organs and personnel in Sinkiang, China, to carry out large-scale subversive activities in the Ili region and enticed and coerced several tens of thousands of Chinese citizens into going to the Soviet Union. The Chinese Government lodged repeated protests and made repeated representations, but the Soviet Government refused to repatriate these Chinese citizens on the pretext of "the sense of Soviet legality" and "humanitarianism." To this day, the incident remains unsettled. This is indeed an astounding event, unheard of in the relations between socialist countries.

5

SOVIET COUNTERCHARGES

(Excerpt from Soviet Government Statement, Tass Information Service, Moscow, September 20, 1963.)

In recent years, the Chinese side has been stooping to acts on the borders with neighboring states that would give reason to think that in this question the PRC [People's Republic of China] Government is departing more and more from Leninist positions. The PRC leaders, deliberately concentrating the people's attention on frontier problems, artificially fan up nationalistic passions and dislike for other peoples.

Beginning with 1960, Chinese servicemen and civilians have been systematically violating the Soviet border. In the single year of 1962, more than 5,000 violations of the Soviet border from the Chinese side were registered. Attempts are also being made to "develop" some parts of Soviet territory without permission.

The Soviet Government has a number of times suggested to the PRC Government that consultations be held on the question of determining separate sections of the border so as to exclude any possibility of misunderstanding. However, the Chinese side evades such consultations, at the same time continuing to violate the border. This cannot but make us wary, especially in view of the fact that Chinese propaganda is making definite hints at the unjust demarcation of some of the sections of the Sino-Soviet border allegedly made in the past.

However, the artificial creation of any territorial problems, especially between socialist countries, would be tantamount to embarking on a very dangerous path. If states now begin to make territorial claims on one another, using as arguments some ancient data and the graves of their forefathers, if they start fighting for the revision of historically developed frontiers, this will lead to no good, merely creating feuds among all the peoples, to the joy of the enemies of peace.

It must not be forgotten that in the past the question of territorial disputes and claims has often been the source of acute friction and conflicts between states, a source of the flaming of nationalistic passions. It is common knowledge that territorial disputes and frontier conflicts were used as a pretext for wars of seizure. That is why Communists consistently work for the solution of frontier problems through negotiations. The socialist countries, guided by the principle of proletarian internationalism in their relations, should show other peoples an example of friendly solution of territorial problems.

6

KHRUSHCHEV ON THE PEACEFUL SETTLEMENT OF BORDER DISPUTES

(Excerpts from message from Premier Khrushchev to the other heads of state regarding the settlement of territorial disputes; text broadcast by Tass International Service, Moscow, January 3, 1964.)

N. S. Khrushchev, Chairman of the Council of Ministers of the USSR, on December 31, 1963 sent the following message to the heads of states—or governments—of the countries of the world:

I am sending you this message in order to draw your attention to one of the problems which, in my opinion, is of particularly great significance for strengthening peace—the question of territorial disputes between countries and the ways of settling them.

. . .

I think that you will agree with me that if we try to pick out the questions which most often give rise to dangerous friction between states in different parts of the world, these undoubtedly will be territorial disputes, the problems of frontiers between states, mutual or unilateral claims of states to each other's territory. . . .

The question of boundaries or, to be more specific, of territorial claims and disputes is not new, of course. It has existed practically through the entire history of humanity and not infrequently caused sharp conflicts between states, mutual mistrust, and enmity among peoples.   . . .

The question before us is how to deal with territorial disputes and claims which arise over the presently existing well-established frontiers of states. Let us have a look, first of all, into the nature of these disputes and claims.

In a special class among such claims are demands of the revenge-seeking circles of certain states which were the aggressors in World War II. These circles, craving revenge for the lost war, are harboring plans for a revision of the just postwar territorial settlement. In the first place, they want to get hold of those territories which went to other states by way of eliminating the consequences of the aggression and providing guarantees of security for the future. Such territorial "claims" must be resolutely rejected as incompatible with the interests of peace, because nothing but a new world war may grow out of these claims.

There exist, however, other territorial claims and border disputes, and they are perhaps the more numerous. These disputes have nothing to do with the postwar settlement. To justify their claims, the parties to these disputes advance arguments and considerations relating to history, ethnography, blood affinity, religion, and so forth.

It often happens that one state justifies by such arguments its territorial claim to another state, and the latter in turn finds other arguments of the same kind but of an absolutely opposed nature, and itself advances a territorial counterclaim. The result is the kindling of passions and deepening of mutual strife. . . .

In many cases, references to history are of no help. Who can affirm that, say, a reference to the seventeenth century which one state puts forward in substantiation of its territorial claim is more valid than, for instance, the reference to the eighteenth or nineteenth century by which the other state tries to bolster its counterclaim? And if one were to take as the basis for the solution of a border dispute the entire history spread over several millennia, all would agree, one should think, that in many cases no real solution could be found. . . .

Occasionally, it is difficult to get one's bearings among numerous "arguments" based on national, ethnographic, or blood-affinity grounds. The development of mankind was such that some peoples are now living on the territories of several states. On the other hand, there exist states of the multinational type inhabited sometimes by dozens of peoples belonging even to different races.

Unfortunately, disputes about borders take place not only between historians and ethnographers but also between states, each of which possesses armed forces—and quite big ones sometimes. . . . This means that one has to display due understanding of boundaries as they have been formed in the course of history.

. . .

And is it not dangerous for the peoples of Asia to use force for the purposes of revising the state borders existing in this part of the world? Of course, they don't need that. Is it not a fact that the border conflicts existing between some states of Asia even now have a most adverse effect on their life? The peoples of the Asian continent face great tasks. It is exceedingly important for them to raise their national economy, lay the groundwork for a modern industry, bring about a turning point in the efficiency of their agriculture, so as to deliver the population of their countries from age-old poverty and want. This calls for great efforts and, above all, for peace and tranquillity on the borders. Now that border conflicts not only exist but sometimes are even aggravated between Asian states, they are compelled to maintain and even increase their armed forces and spend their resources unproductively. Who is to profit from this? Certainly not the peoples of the countries which have liberated themselves from colonial oppression.

. . .

I do not know what words I should choose, but it is my desire to express with utmost clarity the thought that there are not nor can there be such territorial disputes in our time between the already formed states, such unresolved frontier questions, for the solution of which it is permissible to use armed force. No, this cannot be allowed to happen, and we must do everything possible to rule out the possibility of such a development of events. . . .

In all current frontier disputes between states, the sides must of course study the matter thoroughly in order to settle these issues. We are wholly for this. The only thing we are against is the military method of solving territorial disputes. This is what we should agree upon, precisely upon this.

. . .

Considering this, the Soviet Government, guided by the interests of strengthening peace and preventing war, is submitting the following proposal to the consideration of the governments of all states: to conclude an international agreement—or treaty—on the renunciation by states of the use of force for the solution of territorial disputes or questions of frontiers. In our opinion, such an agreement should include the following principal propositions:

First, a solemn undertaking by the states that are parties to the agreement not to resort to force to alter existing state frontiers;

Second, recognition that the territory of states should not even temporarily be the object of any invasion, attack, military occupation, or any other forcible measure directly or indirectly undertaken by other states for whatever political, economic, strategic, frontier, or other considerations;

Third, a firm declaration that neither differences in social or political system, nor denial of recognition or the absence of diplomatic relations, nor any other pretexts can serve as a justification for the violation by one state of the territorial integrity of another;

Fourth, an undertaking to settle all territorial disputes exclusively by peaceful means, such as negotiations, mediation, conciliatory procedures, and also other peaceful means at the option of the parties concerned in accordance with the UN Charter.

Needless to say, such an international agreement should cover all territorial disputes as to the existing borders between states. . . .

Sincerely,

[signed] N. Khrushchev

Chairman of the USSR Council
of Ministers

7

CHOU EN-LAI TO EDGAR SNOW

(Excerpt from Edgar Snow's interview with Chou En-lai, Premier of the State Council of the People's Republic of China, in Conakry, Guinea, January 23, 1964, *New York Times*, February 3, 1964, p. 3.)

Q.—Do you have any serious frontier disputes with the USSR or may one regard existing boundaries as satisfactory to both parties and not subject to future negotiations?

A.—We have reached an agreement with the Soviet Union that negotiations be held on the Sino-Soviet boundary questions.

8

BORDER TALKS REPORTED

(A dispatch from Tanyug International Service, Belgrade, February 27, 1964.)

PEKING—It has been learned here that a delegation of Soviet experts on frontier questions has arrived in Peking to discuss certain matters of common interest. The Soviet delegation arrived in Peking on February 23. So far, they have had one meeting with Chinese representatives at which questions of procedure were discussed.

9

THE CCP TO THE CPSU

(Excerpt from the "Letter of the Central Committee of the Chinese Communist Party of February 29, 1964, to the Central Committee of the Communist Party of the Soviet Union," *Peking Review*, No. 19, May 8, 1964.)

1. The Question of the Sino-Soviet Boundary

The government of the People's Republic of China has consistently held that the question of the boundary between China and the Soviet Union, which is a legacy from the past, can be settled through negotiation between the two Governments. It has also held that, pending such a settlement, the *status quo* on the border should be maintained. This is what we have done for the past ten years or more. Had the Soviet Government taken the same attitude, both sides could have lived in amity along the border and preserved tranquillity there.

With the stepping up of anti-Chinese activities by the leaders of the CPSU in recent years, the Soviet side has made frequent breaches of the *status quo* on the border, occupied Chinese territory and provoked border incidents. Still more serious, the Soviet side has flagrantly carried out large-scale subversive activities in Chinese frontier areas, trying to sow discord among China's nationalities by

37

means of the press and wireless, inciting China's minority nationalities to break away from their motherland, and inveigling and coercing tens of thousands of Chinese citizens into going to the Soviet Union. Not only do all these acts violate the principles guiding relations between socialist countries, they are absolutely impermissible even in the relations between countries in general.

Among all our neighbors it is only the leaders of the CPSU and the reactionary nationalists of India who have deliberately created border disputes with China. The Chinese Government has satisfactorily settled complicated boundary questions, which were legacies from the past, both with all its fraternal socialist neighbors, except the Soviet Union, and with its nationalist neighbors such as Burma, Nepal, Pakistan, and Afghanistan, with the exception of India.

The delegations of our two Governments started boundary negotiations in Peking on February 25, 1964. Although the old treaties relating to the Sino-Russian boundary are unequal treaties, the Chinese Government is nevertheless willing to respect them and take them as the basis for a reasonable settlement of the Sino-Soviet boundary question. Guided by proletarian internationalism and the principles governing relations between socialist countries, the Chinese Government will conduct friendly negotiations with the Soviet Government in the spirit of consultation on an equal footing and mutual understanding and mutual accommodation. If the Soviet side takes the same attitude as the Chinese Government, the settlement of the Sino-Soviet boundary question, we believe, ought not to be difficult, and the Sino-Soviet boundary will truly become one of lasting friendship.

10

A SOVIET CHARGE OF BORDER VIOLATIONS

(Excerpt from a dispatch from Information Service of India, New Delhi, April 8, 1964.)

Soviet Consul General in Calcutta Voinov has accused the Chinese leaders of indulging in adventurism and provoking border incidents with neighboring countries. Speaking at a function on April 7, Voinov said that the violations of the Soviet border by the Chinese in 1962 and 1963 were a constant occurrence. Sometimes this took the form of flagrant provocations.

11

A SOVIET JURIST'S COMMENTS ON THE DISPUTE

(A dispatch from Tass International Service, Moscow, in Russian, April 8, 1964.)

Moscow—"Facts show that the Chinese leaders, following unworthy aims, have set out on the road of undermining the foundations of the socialist camp," well-known Soviet international jurist Fedor Kozhevnikov declared.

"In its policy of petty-bourgeois adventurism and great-power chauvinism, the Chinese leadership has overstepped all limits, openly scorning not only the principles of socialist internationalism but even the basic principles of international law and international morality."

Among the generally accepted principles and standards of this law, for example, are observance of voluntary international obligations, peaceful settlement of disputes, including those concerning frontiers, respect for sovereignty, and the impermissibility of interference in the internal affairs of other countries. "The PRC leaders are clearly ignoring these principles," Kozhevnikov stressed.

Since 1958, the PRC Government has more and more frequently been carrying out various measures undermining Soviet-Chinese friendship, based upon the 1950 treaty [i.e., the Sino-Soviet Treaty of Friendship, Alliance, and Mutual Assistance].

"It is known," Kozhevnikov said, "that no territorial questions exist between the USSR and the PRC and that the Soviet-Chinese frontier has taken shape historically. The only question can be one of separate clarifications of the frontier, which are necessary. But the Chinese side has for some time been continually and systematically violating the Soviet-Chinese frontier and, furthermore, frequently in a crude and provocative manner." The jurist stressed that this "is in flagrant contradiction of the generally accepted standards of law."

"The position of the PRC leaders, which admits to the possibility that half of mankind could perish [in a nuclear war], allegedly in the name of the struggle for a better future, is a deeply amoral one,"

39

Kozhevnikov declared. "The refusal of the PRC Government to take part in the Moscow Test-Ban Treaty cannot be justified in any way."

Kozhevnikov noted that the Soviet people "are firmly convinced of the justice of our noble ideas and unshakably believe that the world Communist movement will overcome the existing difficulties and that the historic mission of the building of Communism will be successfully carried out."

12

THE SUBVERSION IN SINKIANG

(Excerpts from a dispatch from New China News Agency, Peking, International Service, April 28, 1964.)

URUMCHI, April 28—The first session of the Third People's Congress of the Sinkiang Uighur Autonomous Region, recently held in Urumchi, reviewed the past year's work and endorsed the region's 1964 economic plan. The session condemned the modern revisionists for their surreptitious, subversive activities against Sinkiang.

. . .

In the past few years, the authorities of the Soviet Union have violated the principles governing relations between socialist countries, carried out large-scale subversive activities against Sinkiang, enticed and coerced tens of thousands of Chinese citizens into going to the Soviet Union, and created trouble on the border.

The Soviet authorities used their propaganda machine, the press, and the radios in Alma Ata, Tashkent, and Frunze, adjacent to Sinkiang,* to spread lies and slanders, attacking the leadership of the Chinese Communist Party and distorting the history of Sinkiang, in an attempt to undermine the unity of the Chinese people of various nationalities. Saifudin [Chairman of the Sinkiang Uighur Autonomous Region] stressed continued vigilance against modern revisionism.

. . .

Deputies speaking at the session testified to the very favorable situation in Sinkiang and its tremendous achievements in the past

* See Map 1, p. 12. (*Note:* All footnotes are the editor's.)

40

year. They expressed extreme indignation at the Soviet authorities' subversive activities and, drawing conclusions from their personal experience, repudiated the Soviet lies and slanders. All the deputies expressed their determination to strengthen unity and raise their vigilance against the plots of modern revisionism.

13

PRAVDA ON THE SITUATION IN HONG KONG

(Excerpts from a dispatch from Tass International Service, Moscow, May 27, 1964.)

Moscow—British colonialism and Peking's foreign policy are getting along amicably in Hong Kong, the very same [foreign] policy which lays claim to be a model of revolutionism. . . . It would be vain to search in the Peking press for angry words of protest and condemnation of the rule of the colonialists who exploit several million Chinese in Hong Kong. "Uncompromising" whenever the oppressed in other countries are the issue, the Peking press displays amazing indifference to the lot of the unfortunates living in junks or huts in Hong Kong.

[The *Pravda* correspondents report that, according to a Hong Kong newspaper] . . . Peking is annually receiving, on the average, US $300,000,000 from Hong Kong. In the last several years, about 75,000 tons of rice a year and large quantities of meat, fruit, sugar, and fats have been exported from China to Hong Kong. China is also making a big profit from the sale of drinking water, which is in short supply in Hong Kong's working-class section.

The *Pravda* correspondents point out that in recent years capital from the People's Republic of China has been increasingly [used to] penetrate various firms, enterprises, banks, and restaurants in Hong Kong, often gaining full control of them. "How can one speak of class struggle and revolutionary irreconcilability if capital from the People's Republic of China is peacefully collaborating with British and American capital in Hong Kong, jointly exploiting the working people?"

41

14

MAO'S STATEMENT TO THE
JAPANESE SOCIALIST DELEGATION

(Excerpts from "Chairman Mao Tse-tung Tells the Delegation of the Japanese Socialist Party that the Kuriles Must Be Returned to Japan," *Sekai Shūhō*, Tokyo, August 11, 1964.)

On July 10, a five-man group of parliamentary deputies, headed by Kozo Sasaki, from . . . the Japanese Socialist Party had a lengthy talk in Peking with Mao Tse-tung, Chairman of the Chinese Communist Party. In the course of this talk, Mao Tse-tung declared that he "supported the position of Japan on the question of the return of the Kuriles." After arriving in Hong Kong on July 12, the group told this to a group of Japanese correspondents accredited there. The contents of the talk deserve special attention.

. . .

Chairman Mao Tse-tung bitterly criticized the Soviet Union for its territorial ambitions. In appraising this statement, however, we must keep in mind that it was made amid circumstances that have brought diplomatic relations between the two countries to the point of rupture.

. . .

The Sino-Soviet dispute: Touching upon the so-called Sino-Soviet dispute, Mao spoke about the question of Soviet military assistance to India, the recall of Soviet specialists and technicians from China [in July of 1960], etc. Having pointed out that "relations between us and the Soviet Union have become worse and worse since the Twentieth Congress of the CPSU in 1956," he then declared:

"We have been challenged and we are resisting. It has been proposed to us that we stop the open discussion, if even for three months. We have told them we will not stop even for so many days. We have waged war for twenty-five years. Of these twenty-five years, twenty-two years were taken up by the Civil War and the war against Japan, three years by the Korean War. In the past, [although] I was a teacher, I did not know what war was. Three teachers taught me what war was. The first was Chiang Kai-shek, the second was Japanese imperialism, and the third was American imperialism. War is a well-known phenomenon; when it is waged, people die. During these twenty-five years of war, the Chinese people lost several tens of millions of dead and wounded. As regards war on paper, there are no dead in such a war. We have been waging such a war for several years now, and not a single person has died. We are prepared to wage this war for another twenty-five years. The Rumanian delegation [that recently visited China] proposed that we end the dispute. However, as soon as the delegation returned home, Rumania started fighting with the Soviet Union. What is the crux of the matter? The crux lies in the fact that a certain large country is trying to control a number of smaller countries. When one country tries to control another, the latter will resist without fail. Now two large powers—i.e., the United States and the Soviet Union—are trying to become friends and take over control of the whole world. How can we approve of such a development?"

The territorial question: The head of the delegation of the staff of the Socialist Party on the island of Hokkaido, Tetsuo Ara, asked, "At a time when we were kept in ignorance, the Kuriles were taken away from us in accordance with the Yalta Agreement and the Potsdam Declaration. We demand their return [by the Soviet Union] and, in this connection, would like to hear Chairman Mao's opinion."

The following was said in reply: "There are too many places occupied by the Soviet Union. In accordance with the Yalta Agreement, the Soviet Union, under the pretext of assuring the independence of Mongolia, actually placed the country under its domination. Mongolia takes up an area which is considerably greater than the Kuriles. In 1954, when Khrushchev and Bulganin came to China, we took up this question but they refused to talk to us. They [i.e., the Soviet Union] also appropriated part of Rumania. Having cut off a portion of East Germany, they chased the local inhabitants into West Germany. They detached a part of Poland, annexed it to the Soviet Union, and gave a part of East Germany to Poland as compensation. The same thing took place in Finland. The Russians took everything they could. Some people have declared that the Sinkiang area and the territories north of the Amur River must be included in the Soviet Union. The Soviet Union is concentrating troops along its border.

"The Soviet Union has an area of 22 million square kilometers and its population is only 220 million. It is about time to put an end to this allotment. Japan occupies an area of 370,000 square kilo-

43

meters and its population is 100 million. About a hundred years ago, the area to the east of [Lake] Baikal became Russian territory, and since then Vladivostok, Khabarovsk, Kamchatka, and other areas have been Soviet territory.* We have not yet presented our account for this list. In regard to the Kurile Islands, the question is clear as far as we are concerned—they must be returned to Japan."

15

A JAPANESE COMMENT ON MAO'S STATEMENT

(Excerpts from "[Mao Tse-tung Provides] Support for the Reversion of the South Kurile Islands," *Yomiuri Shimbun*, Tokyo, July 13, 1964.)

The news report that Chairman Mao Tse-tung of the Chinese Communist Party expressed to the Japanese Socialist Party's mission to Communist China his stand supporting Japan's request for reversion of the South Kuriles, while bringing out the problem of Soviet territory—including Outer Mongolia, the area north of the Amur River, and a part of East Europe—can be said to be very important in the sense of predicting the future course of the Sino-Soviet conflict. Territorial disputes are the most dangerous factor from the standpoint of international relations. This is because, if such disputes were to be squarely taken up, it would inevitably bring about an extreme worsening of relations between the nations involved. When we look at the fact that this time Chairman Mao himself mentioned the problem, although his opinions have previously been expressed repeatedly in newspapers or treatises, we feel that Sino-Soviet relations have become much worse [as a result]. . . .

Chairman Mao cited the example of Outer Mongolia and other areas in emphasizing that the Soviet Union has been too avaricious in regard to the acquisition of territory. It is said that Communist China is secretly hoping to recover the area north of the Amur River, lost under the 1858 Treaty of Aigun, and even the Maritime Province of Siberia, lost under the 1860 Treaty of Peiping. In Eastern Europe, moreover, it is reported from some quarters that Rumania, which is beginning to follow an "independent line," has asked the USSR for reversion of the Bessarabian area. It is rumored that, if this

---

* See Map 1, p. 12.

44

is true, the USSR may be in a tight spot, particularly because similar problems exist with Poland and Czechoslovakia. The point to be noted particularly at this time is that Chairman Mao reportedly revealed that Rumania has resisted Moscow ever since the Chinese side fully explained its stand to the Rumanian delegation, including Premier Maurer, when it visited Peiping to mediate the Sino-Soviet conflict. It can be said that this statement virtually confirms the fact that Peiping has openly aggravated the friction between the USSR and Eastern Europe on the territorial question.

Thus, the Sino-Soviet conflict has come to assume an aspect close to a mud-slinging contest, with the two nations trying to develop the situation to the advantage of their respective sides through capitalizing not only on the territorial issue between themselves but also on the territorial questions of other countries. However, both Moscow and Peiping are aiming at strengthening their own respective positions to the end. Therefore, the countries cited as examples in this connection should see to it that they are not heedlessly dragged into the Sino-Soviet dispute.

16

AN INTERVIEW WITH CHOU EN-LAI

(Excerpts from report of an interview with Premier Chou En-lai by Okada, Socialist member of the Diet, in *Asahi Shimbun*, Tokyo, August 1, 1964.)

At the interview with Premier Chou En-lai held on July 19, Premier Chou stated as follows:

1. There were some incorrect comments by the Japanese press concerning Chairman Mao Tse-tung's statement. Japan should take care to accept Chinese support of Japan's demand for retrocession of the Kurile Islands. . . . The USSR is holding a large amount of territory which was taken from others since the Czarist period, and it is logical and justifiable for newly independent countries to claim their former territories.

2. At the interview with Premier Khrushchev in January 1957, I requested that the USSR make proper arrangements for the territorial issues covering Japan, China, the Middle East, and the Eastern European countries including Finland. I could not get a satisfactory

45

answer from him then, but the announcement of the issue was kept secret because the Sino-Soviet dispute was not public at that time.

17

ADZHUBEI ON THE DISPUTE

(Excerpt from an interview with Alexei Adzhubei, Khrushchev's son-in-law and then editor of *Izvestia*, by Botho Kirsch and Georg Wolff, in *Der Speigel*, Hamburg, August 2, 1964.)

Q.—Red China, too, is making efforts to enter into business relations with the Federal Republic [i.e., West Germany]. Now it is the case that the Soviet Union finds itself in an ideological dispute with Peking. Does this conflict have any bearing on the German policy of the Soviet Union?

A.—First, we do not have a conflict with the People's Republic of China but with the leaders of the Chinese Communist Party.

Q.—But this is all the same, is it not?

A.—To you, perhaps, but not to us. We insist on our point of view.

Q.—It is known that the Chinese have raised territorial claims against the Soviet Union. What has this to do with ideology?

A.—I would like to quote our Premier, who has said that the borders of our country, west and east, north and south, are sacred. We are prepared to handle all border problems calmly. But one should know also that on the Soviet borders not only our entire military power but also the hearts of all our people stand on guard—in the west as in the east. Our borders are inviolable.

18

IZVESTIA ON THE FRONTIER OF EASTERN EUROPE

(Excerpt from a dispatch from Tass International Service, Moscow, August 10, 1964.)

Moscow—The *Izvestia* of August 10 printed a second feature by Soviet journalists Adzhubei, Lednev, Polyanov, and Pralnikov who visited the German Federal Republic at the invitation of three West German newspapers.

"During many . . . talks in West Germany," they write, "more than once we had to discuss the postwar frontiers of European states. It is known that the question of frontiers is a very complex one. . . ."

The authors further recall that it was the Soviet Government which put this question on a definitely realistic basis and is doing everything in its power for the peaceful settlement of frontier disputes between states.

"But there are 'border problems,'" the authors point out, "which cannot be the subject of political talks or of a political deal. This refers primarily to the frontiers which took shape in Europe after World War II. But then, this also refers to all our frontiers as a whole. There can be no appeal to sentimentality on this matter. Here justice triumphs, which is expressed for us in the single word which will be remembered all our lives—victory."

19

PRAVDA ON MAO'S STATEMENT OF JULY 10

(Editorial, "In Connection with Mao Tse-tung's Talk with a Group of Japanese Socialists," *Pravda*, September 2, 1964; also broadcast over Tass International Service, Moscow, September 1, 1964.)

Mao Tse-tung's talk with a group of Japanese socialists who visited Peking was recently published in Japan. The bourgeois newspapermen lauded his statements to the sky: they liked what the CCP Chairman had said. The content of the conversation was such that at first it was difficult to believe it was authentic. Indeed, bourgeois newspapers may write all sorts of things in an effort to poison the international atmosphere and to provoke quarrels between socialist countries.

It could be expected that Peking would refute this report, but no denial was forthcoming. On the contrary, Chinese leaders have made it clear that Mao Tse-tung's interview published by the Japanese press did take place. The Soviet representative in Peking asked PRC Deputy Minister of Foreign Affairs Wang Ping-nan for an explanation and the latter declared, "If Mao Tse-tung said that, I agree with him." On August 1, the Japanese newspaper *Asahi* published a statement by Chou En-lai. This statement actually contained the same ideas as Mao Tse-tung's interview. Consequently, no doubt was left that the Japanese press was reproducing a true statement of the CCP Chairman.

This interview reveals the aims and positions of the Chinese leadership which they had spoken only in subdued voices so far. It is therefore useful to publish this talk so that the Soviet people can see how far the CCP leaders have gone in their struggle against our people, the peoples of other socialist countries, and the entire world Communist movement.

It is well known that the Chinese leadership, having started their struggle against the CPSU and other Marxist-Leninist parties, have been trying to present the matter as if they were coming out in defense of Marxism-Leninism and "safeguarding" the interests of the world revolutionary and liberation movement. More than that, the CCP leaders did not hesitate to allege that when vilifying our party and our country and speaking about the "bourgeois degeneration of the Soviet people," they were concerned for the interests of our country and of other socialist countries.

When in 1960 the CCP leaders started a polemic dealing with the character of our epoch, the possibility of preventing world war, and peaceful and nonpeaceful transition to socialism and other questions, one could have thought they disagreed with the CPSU and other Marxist-Leninist parties on ideological problems only. But as they were developing the polemic, more and more doubts appeared: Do the CCP leaders really believe what they write? The unseemly political aims of the CCP leaders became more and more clearly discernible behind theoretical controversies. Mao Tse-tung's talk provides another confirmation of this.

It can be seen from the interview with the CCP Chairman that the Chinese leaders no longer even attempt to camouflage their expansionist aspirations. According to the Japanese press, Mao Tse-tung does not even mention ideological questions. In his talk there is not a single word about Marxism-Leninism, about socialism, about the unity of the working class, about the struggle for the interests of the world workers' and national liberation movement. In this talk there is not a trace of the class analysis of the contemporary world, of a class approach to the choice of friends and allies in the struggle against imperialism. The main concern of Mao Tse-tung is to whip up anti-Soviet feelings and to play on the nationalist sentiments of the most reactionary forces.

Mao Tse-tung described the struggle waged by the CCP leader-

48

ship against the Soviet Union and other socialist countries as a "paper war," and added that such a war does no one any harm since no one is killed in it. This, first of all, implies recognition of the fact that the Chinese leaders regard their polemic with the CPSU and other fraternal parties as "a kind of war." Secondly, this clearly reveals the supercilious attitude of the CCP leaders toward the interests of the unity of the world Communist and national liberation movements.

The Communists of the world express their deep concern over the situation that has taken shape in the international Communist movement through the fault of the Chinese leaders. The damage that they have inflicted on the cause of the people's struggle for peace, national independence, and social progress is obvious to everyone. And yet Mao Tse-tung declares: No reason to worry. This is a war without anyone being killed, without casualties! No, we cannot agree with the Chinese leaders' assessment of their own actions. Their struggle against the CPSU, the world Communist movement, and the USSR and other socialist countries is not a "paper war." Insofar as its fierceness, scale, and methods are concerned, it does not differ from the imperialist cold war against the socialist countries.

Mao Tse-tung's pronouncements on the territorial question patently show how far the Chinese leaders have gone in the "cold war" against the Soviet Union. He is not only claiming this or that part of Soviet territory, but is portraying his claims as a part of some "general territorial question." We are faced with an openly expansionist program with far-reaching pretensions.

This program did not appear just today or yesterday. In 1954, a textbook on modern history was published in the PRC with a map of China showing it as it was, in the opinion of its authors, before the First Opium War [of 1839–1842]. This map included as parts of China: Burma, Vietnam, Korea, Thailand, Malaya, Nepal, Bhutan, and Sikkim. In the north, the border ran along the Stanovik Mountain Range, cutting off the Maritime Provinces from the USSR. In the west, parts of Kirghizia, Tadzhikstan, and Kazakhstan up to Lake Balkhash were also included in China. Sakhalin also was shown as Chinese territory. If one is to believe the textbook, all these lands and countries were "state territory of China" and had been taken away from it.

49

At that time, it seemed that publication of such a textbook was the result of laxity or the provocative activities of nationalistic elements. However, subsequent events refuted this conjecture. Maps showing various parts of the Soviet Union and other countries neighboring China as Chinese territory continued to be published in the PRC. Chinese representatives recently began mentioning with increasing frequency hundreds of thousands of square kilometers of Soviet territory which allegedly belong "by right" to China. The recent issue of the Peking magazine *Li-shih Yen-chiu* [Historical Research], No. 4, 1964, contends that Russia allegedly "captured vast lands to the north of the Amur River and to the east of the Ussuri River and annexed at various times vast territories in Sinkiang and in the northeast area."*

Now Mao Tse-tung declared in his interview: "About a hundred years ago the area to the east of [Lake] Baikal became the territory of Russia and from then on Vladivostok, Khabarovsk, Kamchatka, and other points are the territory of the Soviet Union. We have not yet presented our account for this list."

By what right, however, are the Chinese leaders claiming lands that do not belong to China? They refer to the fact that, hundreds of years ago, Chinese troops came to these areas and that the Chinese Emperor at one time collected tribute from the local people. Indeed, were not such a serious question involved, such "historic arguments" could not be called other than childish.

The history of mankind is full of examples of the rise and fall of states and the migration of peoples, during which time the borders between states changed more than once. By resorting to the method of "historic references" on the question of borders, one can prove anything. For instance, one can prove that England is French territory because she was once the possession of the Duke of Normandy. One can prove, on the contrary, that France is an English possession because, during the Hundred Years War, she was nearly completely conquered by the English. With the help of such arguments, one

* The article in question is Liu Ta-nien, "Imperialist Aggression against China and the Anti-Imperialist Struggle of the Chinese People—From the Sino-English Opium War of 1840 to the Founding of the People's Republic of China in 1949," *Li-shih Yen-chiu*, No. 4, July 1964, pp. 101–18. Liu also criticized the fact that, in 1911, "Russia sent her troops to enter Urga [Ulan Bator] and supported the Outer Mongolian princes in organizing an 'independent government.'"

can also prove the PRC borders pass only along the line of the Great
Wall of China which is less than 100 kilometers away from Peking.
Indeed, the border of China did once pass there and the wall itself
is testimony of this.

But even if one takes the references to "historic rights" seriously,
it will come out that in this case they do not correspond in any way
to the facts. It is well known that in the middle of the seventeenth
century China's possessions reached only to the Khingan Mountain
Range, i.e., considerably to the south of the Amur River. The territories to the north of Khingan were populated by local indigenous
tribes—Evenks, Daurs, and so forth—who were subjected from time
to time to raids by the Manchu and paid tribute to them. There was
no indigenous Manchu and Chinese population in the Amur Valley.
The process of the definition of actual borders took place with the
annexation by Russia of the northern half of the Amur Basin and of
the southern part by China. More than a hundred years ago, this
state of the border was fixed in the Aigun and Peking treaties.

No one disagrees: the Czarist Government carried out a preda-
tory policy, just as the Chinese Emperors carried one out themselves
to the extent of their abilities. At various times, now one side now
the other was stronger and took the upper hand over the adversary.
This resulted in a certain change in the settlement of peoples. But
the common people did not think about any territorial gains. They
worked on the land they had to live on, watering it with their sweat.
One can only be amazed that there are people questioning the right
of workers and peasants to the land where they have lived and worked
from ancient times solely on the grounds that, once upon a time in
deep antiquity, one Emperor defeated another and then himself suffered defeat.

Have those who question the inclusion in the Soviet Union of a
territory of more than one and a half million square kilometers con-
sidered how these claims will be taken by Soviet people who have
lived and worked on this land for several generations and consider
it their homeland, the land of their ancestors? That is why we say
that the present border has developed historically and was fixed by
life itself, and [past] treaties regarding the border cannot be dis-
regarded.

The CPSU led the struggle of the working class and toiling masses

51

of Russia against Czarism and routed it in the end. It is well known that, in the very first years of its existence, the Soviet Government liquidated all the unequal treaties with China. Continuing its Leninist policy, the Soviet Government gave up the naval base at Port Arthur and handed over, free of charge, to the PRC Government all rights in the joint management of the Chinese Changchun Railway, together with all the property belonging to the railway. V. I. Lenin wrathfully condemned the capture of Port Arthur by the Czarist Government and the infiltration of Manchuria. But it was none other than Lenin who said: "Vladivostok is far away, but this town is ours."

The Soviet Union is an absolutely new state formation which emerged as the result of a voluntary unification of Soviet republics created on the ruins of the Czarist Empire. Whereas the borders of Czarist Russia were determined by the policy of imperialist predators, the borders of the Soviet Union were formed as a result of a voluntary statement of the will of the peoples on the basis of the principle of free self-determination of nations. The peoples which form the Soviet Union will never allow anyone to encroach upon their right to settle their destiny themselves.

In his talk, Mao Tse-tung bemoaned the fate of Mongolia which, he said, was put "under its rule" by the Soviet Union. This can evoke nothing but indignation. Everybody knows that the Mongolian People's Republic has been a sovereign socialist state for more than forty years and enjoys all the rights of an independent country.

Why did Mao Tse-tung have to make such obviously wild statements? The fact is that the existence of an independent Mongolian state, which maintains friendly relations with the USSR and other socialist countries, does not suit the Chinese leaders. They would like to deprive Mongolia of its independence and make it a Chinese province. It was precisely about this that the PRC leaders offered "to reach agreement" with N. S. Khrushchev and other Soviet comrades during their visit to Peking in 1954.*

N. S. Khrushchev naturally refused to discuss this question and told the Chinese leaders that the destiny of the Mongolian people

---

* It should be noted that *Pravda* does not indicate in this editorial the full extent of the territorial claims advanced by Mao Tse-tung on July 10 (see p. 44). Nor is there any mention of the 1957 talks between Khrushchev and Chou En-lai, in which territorial claims were reportedly discussed (see pp. 45–46).

is not determined in Peking or Moscow but in Ulan Bator and that the question of Mongolia's statehood can be settled only by that country's working people and nobody else.

As already noted above, the Chinese leaders are trying to elevate territorial claims to the level of some general principle. However, this involves fundamental points of international relations. What would happen if all states would follow the Peking recipe and begin presenting mutual claims to each other for a revision of historically formed borders? There is no difficulty in answering this question. This road would mean an inevitable aggravation of international tension and be fraught with military conflicts and all the consequences ensuing therefrom.

The question of territorial disputes and borders is tremendously complex. One should evaluate the nature of territorial issues. It is one thing when the matter at hand is the just striving of people to liquidate remnants of the shameful colonial system and get back ancient territories populated by the corresponding nation and held by imperialists. For example, the right of the Indian people to return Goa to the motherland was indisputable. Just as indisputable was Indonesia's right to return West Irian to the Republic. We have declared and continue to declare that People's China has every right to press for the liberation and reunification of Taiwan and Hong Kong, which are a part of the country and the majority of whose population are Chinese. Such examples are numerous.

Territorial claims stemming from attempts to revise historically formed borders between states—to force in any form a revision of treaties and agreements concluded after World War II as a result of the rout of Hitler fascism and Japanese militarism—are quite another thing. People who have won victory at the price of millions upon millions of lives will never agree to such strivings.

In his talk with the Japanese socialists, Mao Tse-tung crossed out with amazing ease the entire system of international agreements concluded after World War II which meet the interests of strengthening peace and the security of people. He declared, "The places occupied by the Soviet Union are too numerous," and even named some territories with the obvious aim of adding inflammatory material to fan nationalistic passions. It is hard to believe that the Chinese leader does not understand the causes and historic circumstances of the present borders between states in Europe and Asia. In addition, it is difficult to believe that he is unaware of the most dangerous consequences that could result from any attempt to recarve the map of the world under present conditions.

Mao Tse-tung pretends to attack the interests of our country only, but it is clear to everyone that such a provocative appeal to revise borders, if taken seriously, would invariably generate a whole series of mutual demands, claims, and insoluble conflicts between countries of Europe and Asia. The self-evident nature of all this cannot be doubted and is cause for stating that only those who find it profitable for some reasons to sow mistrust and animosity between people of socialist countries can act in such a manner.

It is precisely with this aim that Mao Tse-tung is trying to fabricate so-called territorial issues between a number of socialist countries. However, these attempts are doomed to failure in advance. No one will ever succeed in undermining the friendship and cooperation of the people of the socialist countries.

The bosses of the capitalist world have for a long time been watching the nationalism of the Chinese leaders and their great-power manners. It is therefore not fortuitous that representatives of the right wing of the Japanese socialists, too, put the question of the Kurile Islands precisely to Mao Tse-tung and received from the CCP Chairman precisely the answer they wanted. It is known that the transfer of these islands to full possession by the Soviet Union was not at all the result of Soviet expansion, as Mao Tse-tung is trying to contend. This move was dictated by the need to cut short the aggressive policy of Japanese imperialism which, beginning in 1918, harbored plans of capturing Soviet territories in the Far East and repeatedly tried to implement [these plans].

The Kurile Islands played a special role in the aggressive plans of the Japanese militarists—the role of an important beachhead for attacking the Soviet Far East. Naturally, it is quite understandable that the Japanese military had to be deprived of such an opportunity. This was done and, in their time, the Chinese representatives approved this security measure more than once. It was pointed out in the PRC Government statement on August 15, 1951: "The Kurile Islands must be handed over and the southern part of Sakhalin and all its adjacent islands returned to the Soviet Union."

Can one say that the situation in this area has markedly changed since then and that the threat of aggression against the USSR and the other socialist countries has completely ceased to exist? Of course not. Militaristic forces which would like to lead the country along the old road of military adventures are active in Japan, contrary to the will of its people. There are U.S. military bases in Japan which are kept by the Pentagon for certain reasons near the Soviet Union and the other socialist countries of Asia. Only several days ago, the Japanese Government succumbed to U.S. pressure and granted [the United States] the right to send nuclear submarines to Japanese ports; i.e., it permitted the United States to use these ports as military bases. Under these conditions, the statement that the USSR must give the Kurile Islands to Japan plays into the hands of not only the Japanese but also the American militarists.

If we proceed from Mao Tse-tung's so-called historic principle, then all rights to this territory belong to the Soviet Union. However, Chairman Mao is absolutely arbitrary in handling the principles which he himself advances. He refers to them when he finds it profitable and flouts them if this is required by his political plans.

There are not and cannot be any legal or moral grounds for [Japanese] claims to the Kurile Islands. However, this does not mean that the search for solutions that would not impinge upon the interests of the USSR and would meet the needs of the Japanese people would be excluded under changed conditions.

Mao Tse-tung cannot but realize that the Chinese leadership's position on the territorial question is remote from internationalism. To smooth over this impression, he appeals not only to history but also to "justice." His thesis actually boils down to the fact that the population of the world is distributed unevenly and therefore, allegedly, justice demands the reallotment of territory.

The demagogic nature of this thesis is clear to everyone. The distribution of people in the world is a result of a long and complicated development, with the result that different peoples live under different conditions. Communists are fighting precisely to ensure a better life for all people. When socialism triumphs throughout the world and productive forces achieve a higher level everywhere, the process of the *rapprochement* of nations will result in the gradual disappearance of differences in the living conditions of peoples of different countries, and state frontiers will lose their importance. Under these conditions, a solution to the problem of a more even distribution of peoples in the world will become possible.

However, this is a matter for the future. To raise this question now, at a time when opposing systems exist and the objective process of consolidating statehood and sovereignty is under way, is extremely harmful.

Incidentally, it should not be forgotten that history knows many cases when the most reactionary wars were begun with a view to expanding "Lebensraum." Thus, Mao Tse-tung's pronouncements about the "unfair distribution of territory" are not very new. He has predecessors of whom he can scarcely be proud.

Noteworthy also are Mao Tse-tung's statements about the "grandeur" of Japan—statements which are quite surprising coming from a Communist. The great-power views of the CCP leaders and their admiration of the factor of brute force in international relations are clearly discernible in their statements.

Wherein does Mao Tse-tung see the grandeur of the Japanese people? In their industriousness, in the fact that they succeeded in raising their country to the level of the foremost powers of the world within a short space of time and creating a wonderful material and spiritual culture? No, his attention is not attracted by these facts. With extraordinary inspiration, he speaks about the crimes of the Japanese military who in the early forties occupied enormous expanses in Southeast Asia and the Pacific. In other words, Chairman Mao declares the aggressive actions of the Japanese samurai to be Japan's national grandeur, i.e., the actions which the Japanese people themselves regard as a national disgrace.

History teaches us that no country has ever achieved grandeur on the path of military gambles and aggression. The true grandeur of people is reached on the path of social progress, friendship, and cooperation. We are convinced that the vital interests of the Chinese people are also to be found on this path.

All those who cherish the interests of socialism, the preservation of peace, and the security of nations cannot but most emphatically denounce the expansionist views of the PRC leaders and their attempt to gamble with questions which affect the destiny of people.

The true schemes of the Chinese leaders become obvious. These

56

schemes have nothing in common with the interests of the struggle for the victory of the cause of peace and socialism. They are permeated through and through with great-power chauvinism and hegemonism. Mao Tse-tung's talk with the Japanese socialists is the most eloquent and graphic evidence of this.

20

RADIO MOSCOW TO GERMANY

(Excerpt from "Chinese Communist Party Attacks World Peace by Creating a Split," a Radio Moscow broadcast to Germany, in German, by Boris Stolpovski, September 3, 1964.)

The dangerous evolution of the views and practical policies of the Peking leaders is reflected in Mao Tse-tung's conversation with a group of Japanese socialists. This conversation is the embodiment in concentrated form of the irrational lust for war, of nationalism and chauvinism.

The leader of the Chinese Communist Party is now advancing claims against the territory of other states. He is trying to fabricate so-called territorial issues between the socialist countries. Such a provocative call for a revision of frontiers can please only the exponents of the most extremist forces of international reaction. Significantly, elements in militarist circles in Bonn and Japan immediately began to stir—elements long bent upon obtaining a revision of treaties and agreements made at the end of the last war after the smashing of Hitler fascism and Japanese militarism.

21

ANOTHER SOVIET COMMENT ON THE
MAO INTERVIEW

(Excerpts from a round-table discussion of Sino-Soviet relations, Moscow Domestic Service broadcast, in Russian, September 6, 1964.)

What do I consider to be most important [in Mao's interview]? First, the frank admission that the CCP leadership is in practice waging a cold war against the Soviet Union and our Party, and not only is waging one but is ready, as Mao Tse-tung frankly put it, to continue this war for another twenty-five years. Second, the virtual recognition of the permissibility and, to put it bluntly, desirability of considerably revising the borders of the socialist states. This accusation, framed in the spirit of the worst examples of imperialist propaganda, alleges that the Soviet Union is occupying a number of territories. Definite territorial claims are made against the Soviet Union [by the Chinese] and a vast territory is involved—all of the territory of our country east of [Lake] Baikal.

. . .

What is the meaning of raising the question of the supposed duty of the USSR to hand over the Kuriles to Japan? This is open flirtation with Japanese militarism and, in substance, is a proposal . . . for a definite military and political alliance with these circles. I have already mentioned the fact that Mao Tse-tung spoke of a number of territories supposedly "occupied" by the Soviet Union, and he raises directly the question of reviewing the frontiers established in accordance with the decisions of the Yalta and Potsdam conferences. In other words, what is involved is the advancing or support of certain territorial claims which are being made by the West German revanchists. It is these circles alone who openly make such statements about the need to revise frontiers, and so forth. Thus, Mao Tse-tung is keeping very definite company—the company of the Japanese ruling circles, the Japanese militarists, and the West German revanchists.

. . .

After the incorrect points of view and the vicious concepts contained in Mao Tse-tung's conversation had been unmasked so actively, many observers and commentators began to pose the question: what explains the timing of a conversation of this kind between Mao Tse-tung and the Japanese group? Why was it precisely at this time that such a statement was made, a statement which undoubtedly— as *Pravda* has stated—unmasks the views of Mao Tse-tung himself? Why was the statement made at this time?

Here one cannot but agree with those observers who see in this a certain logic, the logic of struggle against the Soviet Union, against the correct position of Marxist-Leninist parties which demands that, should a cold war be declared on the Soviet Union, it is natural and logical to make sure of one's allies. Since Peking cannot find these allies among the Marxist-Leninist parties as it would like to do, it is now seeking these allies among the right-wing revanchist forces.

58

22

RADIO MOSCOW TO ITALY

(Excerpts from "The Expansionist Program of the Chinese Leaders," a Radio Moscow broadcast to Italy, in Italian, by Vladimir Kozyakov, September 6, 1964.)

For some years now, statements have appeared in China in connection with territories which allegedly always belonged to China but [now] form part of neighboring states. In 1954, for example, a school manual on modern history was published in China which included a Chinese geography map. This map showed that Burma, Vietnam, Korea, Thailand, Malaya, Nepal, Bhutan, Sikkim, as well as the Soviet Far East, part of Kirghizia, Tadzhikstan, Kazakhstan, and the island of Sakhalin once belonged to China and were later separated from it.

We in the Soviet Union were at that time inclined to think that this was just the opinion of individuals full of rabid nationalism; in the years that followed, however, Chinese propaganda about territorial claims against neighboring states began to increase. Recently, official Chinese spokesmen started to talk of hundreds of thousands of square kilometers of Soviet territory which supposedly belong by right to China. Now Mao Tse-tung, Chairman of the Chinese Communist Party, and other Chinese leaders are openly advancing claims on territories belonging to other countries and peoples. At his meeting with Japanese socialists, Mao Tse-tung stated explicitly, "About a hundred years ago, the zone to the east of Lake Baikal became Russian territory and since then Vladivostok, Khabarovsk, Kamchatka, and other points have been included in Soviet territory. We have not yet presented our account for this list."

It is thus perfectly clear today that territorial claims against other countries represent part of the official course of the Chinese leaders and are the pivots of an openly expansionist program. And it is quite symptomatic that Mao Tse-tung does not limit the list of Soviet zones to which China is laying claim. In his conversation with the Japanese socialists, he formulated an entire theory referring to the territorial question in general. He indicated various regions in Europe and Asia which in his opinion should belong to other countries. Mao Tse-tung does not pay any attention either to the state frontiers created through history or to the postwar agreements which serve the cause of preserving peace and the security of peoples. Mao Tse-tung is raising territorial claims by one state in respect to another state to the rank of a general principle and seems to want to invite other countries to pursue China's example and to undertake together with it a campaign to revise the world geographical map. And to make this policy hold water theoretically, Mao Tse-tung takes recourse to ancient reasoning about an unequal division of territory among peoples of various countries.

Commenting on the statements by the Chinese leaders, the veteran Communist Fedor Petrov, a Party member since 1896, defined them as a militant anti-Marxist and anti-Leninist concept. "I, as well as my Party colleagues who have been in the rank and file for six decades," Fedor Petrov stated, "know very well where and when a Communist speaks up and when one only pretends to be a Communist." And, in fact, Mao Tse-tung's "pedantry" [*elucubrazione*] in regard to the revision of frontiers created throughout history cannot have anything in common with the opinion of Communists. His reasoning about the unequal division of territory is only a new edition of the theory of "Lebensraum."

To date, the most desperate exponents of imperialism have been conducting a provocative anti-Soviet campaign, accusing the Soviet Union of subjugating other socialist states. But the absurdity of these accusations is so plain that even numerous bourgeois exponents tend to dissociate themselves from this dirty campaign, while the Chinese leaders, however, have accepted openly the anti-Soviet theses of the imperialists.

Up to now, the only European country which has advanced territorial claims against neighboring states has been West Germany. For this, the Bonn leaders earned themselves the fame of being revenge-mongers who threaten the peace and security of the peoples of Europe. Now the Chinese leaders also openly attack the frontiers formed throughout history in Europe, thus promoting a revanchist mood in Japan.

It has long been known that the imperialist states are trying persistently to divide socialist states and spread disagreement and mistrust among them. In this, they reckon above all on the possibility of reviving nationalism and chauvinism. The Chinese leaders are now helping them [to do this] by their increased contribution to the creation of an atmosphere of mistrust and tension in the world. It is to this end that Mao Tse-tung is trying to fabricate so-called territorial questions.

However, by preaching such theories, the Chinese leaders are sawing off the branch on which they are sitting. . . . After Mao Tse-tung's meeting with the group of Japanese socialists, nobody doubts any longer that the Chinese leaders are in fact pursuing tarnished political aims that are dictated by a desire for expansion.

The true designs of the Chinese leaders have come to light, *Pravda* declared in one of its recent editorials. These designs have nothing in common with the struggle for the victory of the cause of peace and socialism. They are riddled throughout with great-power chauvinism and hegemonistic aims. Mao Tse-tung's conversation with the Japanese socialists is the most powerful and obvious proof of this.

23

THE MONGOLIAN GOVERNMENT'S REACTION
TO THE MAO INTERVIEW

(Excerpts from a broadcast from Montsame International Service, Ulan Bator, in Russian, September 10, 1964.)

ULAN BATOR, September 9—On September 9, the Mongolian News Agency—Montsame—transmitted a statement for publication in the press which was broadcast over the Ulan Bator radio. The text of the statement follows:

In connection with the talk between Mao Tse-tung, Chairman of the Central Committee of the Chinese Communist Party, and a group of Japanese socialists which took place in Peking on July 10, 1964, the Mongolian News Agency has been authorized to issue the following statement:

From the Japanese press, the whole world has learned of the statement by Mao Tse-tung which revealed most distinctly certain essential aspects of the real intentions of the Chinese leaders who are carrying on splitting, subversive activities within the Communist movement.

The Chairman of the Central Committee of the CCP presented

a renovated version of the anti-Marxist "theory of the intermediate zone"* aimed, to all intents and purposes, at collusion with the class enemies of socialism, in order to realize the far-reaching nationalistic plans of the Chinese leaders. In his talk, Mao Tse-tung also openly flaunted his expansionist aspirations, laying groundless territorial claims against neighboring socialist countries. It is evident from the talk that the anti-Soviet, antisocialist, subversive activities of the Chinese leaders have already inexorably led them to effect a great retreat away from Marxism-Leninism and toward a *rapprochement* with the most reactionary, counterrevolutionary forces.

Having entered upon this extraordinarily dangerous path, the Chinese leaders naturally deny the proletarian class approach to social order and substitute their petty-bourgeois, nationalistic concepts. In this respect, on many basic questions they have already long since outdone the most inveterate revisionists ever known in the international Communist movement. In their attempts to redraw the maps of individual countries, the Chinese leaders search for the support of imperialist monopolies and resort, for example, to praise of the aggression of Japanese militarists during World War II.

In the talk, the Chairman of the CCP Central Committee paid particular attention to the Mongolian People's Republic [MPR], whose independent state existence has always been disliked by Chinese nationalists. The Chinese leaders long ago cherished the hope of turning the MPR into a subordinate outlying district of China. As early as 1936, Mao Tse-tung, in a talk with the American writer Edgar Snow, stated that, with the victory of the people's revolution in China, the MPR "will automatically become" a part of China.†

---

* This "theory," advanced by the Chinese Communists, describes the world in terms of a "vast intermediate zone" between the United States and the Soviet Union. The zone is composed of two parts: (1) the emerging states of Asia, Africa, and Latin America and (2) the whole of Western Europe, Australia, Canada, and other "capitalist" states. Those countries in the latter part are said to have a dual character; i.e., their ruling classes are oppressive, yet they are themselves subject to U.S. "oppression" and want to be free of U.S. "control." Thus, it is argued, "they have something in common with the socialist countries." Editorial, "All Forces of the World, Unite to Oppose American Imperialism" (Ch'üan shih-chieh i-ch'ieh fan-tui mei-ti-kuo-chu-i te li-liang lien-ho ch'i-lai), *Jen-min jih-pao,* January 21, 1964.

† Mao's statement is in Edgar Snow's *Red Star Over China* (New York: Modern Library, 1944), p. 96.

This statement of Mao Tse-tung attests to the crudity and obvious disregard which the Chinese leaders have for the fate of peoples. As we can see, he had at that time already personally "decided" the fate of the Mongolian state without the consent of the Mongolian people. And following the founding of the Chinese People's Republic, Mao Tse-tung and other Chinese leaders continued their repeated attempts to decide the fate of our people and, through behind-the-back methods, to include the MPR as a part of China.

There is no doubt that the attempts to deprive the MPR of its independent political existence are also designed to serve the realization of Peking's essentially racist and extremely expansionist concepts as expressed in the formula: "The East wind will prevail over the West wind." In the light of the foregoing, the question suggests itself whether it is possible to trust the sincerity of the individual assertions of the Chinese leaders about their respect for the rights and interests of other peoples.

The attempts of the Chinese leaders to make the MPR a province of China, to all intents and purposes, differ in no way from the annexationist policies of the Chinese landowners and militarists and Kuomintang reactionaries who were violent enemies of the sovereignty of the Mongolian people. The Chinese leaders' claim to Mongolia, a state whose history goes back deep into antiquity, is the result of a great-power policy inherited from the Manchus. The dark plans of the Chinese nationalists to do away with the political independence of the MPR are absurd and unattainable.

Everyone knows that the Mongolian people, having accomplished the people's revolution in 1921, gained their freedom through selfless struggle and, on a new foundation, revived the political independence of their country which was lost at the end of the seventeenth century as a result of the foreign expansion of the Manchu and Chinese conquerors. The MPR, which has developed for more than forty years as a sovereign people's democratic state, has received wide international recognition and has established and developed friendly relations and cooperation with scores of countries throughout the world. Our people, having achieved outstanding successes in socialist construction, are reaping the fruits of their freedom and independent existence and will allow no one to infringe upon their sovereign rights.

In his statement, Mao Tse-tung violently attacked the MPR's

63

friendly relations with the Soviet Union, trying to question the sincerity of these relations. He alleged that "the Soviet Union, under the pretext of protecting the independence of Mongolia, has actually brought the country under its rule." Why has it been necessary for Mao Tse-tung to resort to this shameless slander? Apparently, he is irritated by the fact that the revolutionary achievements of the Mongolian people and their fraternal, inviolable friendship with the Soviet Union stand as an insurmountable obstacle in the path toward the realization of the Peking leaders' dream of transforming Mongolia into a part of China.

The great Soviet Union has always been and remains our true, unselfish friend and reliable protector. It is precisely because of the internationalistic policy and multilateral assistance of the Soviet Union that the Mongolian people were able to defend their freedom and independence from the encroachment of imperialists and to achieve historic successes in increasing the prosperity of their country. . . . Every MPR worker clearly realizes that if our people did not link their destiny with that of the Soviet Union, Mongolia would not be independent and would not have those successes which it has attained. It is clear that if the plans of the Chinese leaders were realized, our people would share the fate of the Inner Mongolians and other national minorities of China who are dealt with on the basis of a policy of great-Han chauvinism. . . .

The slanderous attacks of the Chinese Communist leaders against the friendship of [the Mongolian and Soviet] peoples serve their foul aims of undermining the unity and solidarity of friendly socialist countries and isolating the other socialist countries from the Soviet Union. The adventurist policy and expansionist aspirations of the Chinese leaders will greatly damage the vital interests of the Chinese people and will deter the strengthening of their friendship and cooperation with the peoples of other socialist countries, including the Mongolian people. The great-power views and activities of the Chinese leaders, which are in flagrant contradiction to Marxism-Leninism, show their true character and expose the untruth and hypocrisy of the bombastic allegations in which they assert that they respect the equal rights and sovereignty of other peoples and that they believe in the principles of proletarian internationalism.

Mao Tse-tung's militant chauvinism and crude attacks on the MPR and other socialist countries provoke the profound indignation of the Mongolian people. MPR workers resolutely condemn the great-power, nationalistic views and policies of the Chinese leaders which pursue the adventuristic aims of expansionism and hegemony.

24

MORE SUBVERSION IN SINKIANG

(Excerpts from "Ili's Ten Fruitful Years," *Peking Review*, No. 37, September 11, 1964, pp. 5, 26.)

Bigger crops, more livestock and new, modern industrial plants and mines are some of the many achievements reviewed on the 10th anniversary of the founding of the Ili Kazakh Autonomous *Chou* [District] (in Sinkiang), which borders on the Soviet Union and the Mongolian People's Republic. . . .

One of the most important aspects of the great achievements of the autonomous *chou* was that its people of all nationalities had resolutely repelled the subversive and sabotage activities of the Khrushchev revisionist group, Tan Tung [Vice-Chairman of the Nationalities Affairs Commission of the State Council] said. He described these achievements as a victory for Marxism-Leninism and Mao Tsetung's thinking.

Khrushchev Group's Subversive Activities Denounced. Between August 26–29 the 4th People's Congress of the Ili Kazakh Autonomous *Chou* held its second session in Ining. It heard a report on the work of the *chou* People's Council given by Irhali, the Kazakh chairman of Ili. After reviewing the outstanding successes won by the people of the area on the political and ideological fronts and in all branches of the economy, he noted that these achievements had been made in the course of struggle against sabotage by the Khrushchev revisionist group. . . .

Irhali said that the Khrushchev revisionist group had not accepted defeat. It was attempting new acts of subversion and sabotage. "Since April of this year in particular," he continued, "it has been using its broadcasting services, newspapers, magazines and other propaganda media in a strenuous effort to spread lies slandering the leadership of the Chinese Communist Party. It has been attacking Chairman Mao, the great leader of our people of all nationalities, distorting the history of the Ili Kazakh Autonomous *Chou*, and trying to poison the relations among the various nationalities of this area in order to undermine our national unity."

"Still more outrageous is the fact that the Khrushchev revisionist group has been constantly creating border incidents and attempting to disrupt production in the border areas."

In carrying out these criminal activities, the Khrushchev revisionist group harbored wild ambitions, Irhali pointed out. "We must heighten our vigilance and firmly smash all its schemes for sabotage," the Chairman of the Ili Kazakh Autonomous *Chou* concluded.

In their discussions delegates to the congress representing all the nationalities of the *chou* expressed their satisfaction with the work of the council during the past year. They also indignantly denounced the subversive and sabotage activities of the Khrushchev revisionist group.

Urumhan, a deputy from Yumin County in the Tahcheng region, recalled that in 1962, the Khrushchev revisionist group had incited or coerced a number of people living in the border areas to flee and for a time this had created difficulties for local production. . . . Lately, especially beginning from this year, letters had been received from many of the people who had run away saying that they had been deceived by Khrushchev. . . .

The congress unanimously adopted a resolution declaring that the people of Ili would . . . strive for still greater results and work energetically to smash completely all subversion and sabotage undertaken by the Khrushchev revisionist group.

25

RADIO MOSCOW TO YUGOSLAVIA

(Excerpts from a Radio Moscow broadcast to Yugoslavia, in Serbo-Croatian, by Victor Glazunov, September 15, 1964.)

Before coming to the essence of the problem, I would like to make a slight digression. It seems to me that it would help us to better understand the essence.

There is a West German newspaper called *National Zeitung und Soldaten Zeitung.* This newspaper openly advocates fascist ideas, and its militant appeals embarrass even the Bonn officials. They try to dissociate themselves from this paper, although they do not take any substantial measures against it. This paper has been in raptures of enthusiasm for the Peking leaders recently. The paper was very pleased with the conversation that Mao Tse-tung had with the Japanese socialists. The paper has begun writing on the indispensability of friendship with China, and to make it clear to everybody on what basis [this friendship is to be developed], the paper has published a map displaying on one side the territorial claims of the German Federal Republic and on the other side the Chinese claims.* Thus, they have come closer on the basis of territorial expansionism.

Dear listeners: You have probably noticed that with people who line up for the same aims there are many things they have in common in their expressions as well as in their terminology. This has happened again. Exploring their expansionist program, the Peking leaders speak about unjust distribution of territories. *National Zeitung und Soldaten Zeitung* also speaks about territorial injustice toward Germany. It is quite clear what this paper has in mind. It does not accept the results of World War II and craves revenge, disguising it under reasoning about alleged injustice toward defeated Germany. But what have the Peking leaders in mind when they speak about an unjust distribution of territories and what should justice look like in their opinion?

The Peking leaders say that the world's population is unevenly distributed. The conclusion is drawn from this that it is necessary to redistribute the world's population. But how?

In his conversation with the Japanese socialists, Mao Tse-tung openly declared that this can be done by taking certain territories from one country and handing them over to another. Even if we suppose that this operation is done in a peaceful manner, a number of problems crop up. People live in these territories; these are their native lands; they have toiled the land and erected buildings. Where are these people to be driven to? How is the fruit of their labor to be treated if the soil they live upon, according to Mao Tse-tung, is to be handed over to another state? You cannot simply hand over the people together with the land to another country. This means that they must be moved somewhere. Where to? And will they accept it voluntarily? If they do not, this means that they must be driven away from their native places by force. But what nation would allow its land to be dismembered? The question arises, who is going to be the supreme judge and pass judgment that this or that nation

* *Deutsche National Zeitung und Soldaten Zeitung*, August 21, 1964, p. 1.

has land in abundance or has a shortage? From what country is land to be taken away, and what country is to be added to? How much is to be taken away and how much added?

Under present conditions, when there exist in the world countries with different social systems, and when hostilities prevail in relations between some countries, and when, moreover, there are military blocs of countries directed against each other, talk about injustice in the distribution of territories only helps various aggressive circles which are dreaming of getting rich at other people's expense.

. . .

The appeals for so-called territorial justice can only be taken as a disguise for imperialist aggression. Mao Tse-tung's reasoning in regard to unjustly distributed territories is a Chinese version of the dangerous theory of "Lebensraum." As regards territorial issues, the threat thus leads from Peking by way of the neofascists around the *National Zeitung und Soldaten Zeitung* to the gentlemen of the Third Reich. This is a company of which the Chinese leaders can hardly be proud.

The Peking territorial doctrine is contributing to the aggravation of international tension. It inspires the most aggressive circles, the West German revanchists among them, who are dreaming of the re-distribution of territories. The West German paper *Handelsblatt* [Trade Journal], in welcoming the Chinese leaders' expansionist plans, has, for instance, proclaimed the Oder-Neisse border illegal and has openly demanded that the line should be liquidated. Thus, the Chinese leaders' theories are opening the way for new aggressors who crave warlike adventures.

26

KHRUSHCHEV'S STATEMENT TO A JAPANESE PARLIAMENTARY DELEGATION

(Excerpts from a dispatch from Tass International Service, Moscow, September 19, 1964.)

It can only be regretted that some statesmen sow not the seeds of peace, but seeds of strife and enmity when they meet representatives of other countries. One such "sower" recently talked to Japanese socialists and sowed precisely such seed during his talk. In connection with this, I should like to avail myself of this meeting with you, as members of Parliament and representatives of the Japanese people, to share my views on Mao Tse-tung's pronouncements.

It hurt to read these pronouncements, not only because they are directed against the Soviet Union, against our peoples, our country, but also because Mao Tse-tung calls himself a Communist. But the philosophy which he propounded in the conversation is alien to the working people; it cannot be a philosophy representative of the most progressive, revolutionary teaching—Communism. I am not telling you this to impress my ideas upon you; you know that our Party firmly abides by Marxist-Leninist principles and is sincerely dedicated to this teaching.

Japan and Russia have waged war against each other repeatedly in the past. Japan inflicted a defeat upon Russian Czarism. This was a war between two imperialist powers. During World War II the Soviet Union, together with her allies, inflicted a defeat on the warlike imperialist clique which ruled Japan at that time.

This was the past. What are we to do in the future? We live next door to each other and are neighbors. How are we to cultivate relations between our two countries, between our peoples? Can we follow the old "practice," in which states, having finished one war, immediately started preparations for the next? As a matter of fact, Mao Tse-tung is pushing Japan onto this absolutely incorrect road, [a road] which will not bring happiness to the Japanese people.

When the Japanese socialists raised the question of the Kurile Islands, Mao Tse-tung found nothing better than to say that Japan has such and such a territory and its population is such and such, while the Soviet Union has much more land per capita than Japan and other countries. All the world evaluated this as a provocative discourse. Even the Japanese Government is known to have rejected this reasoning of Mao Tse-tung. Such pronouncements do not contribute to the creation of correct, good relations between the peoples and cannot bring anything good to the peoples.

The "theory" of overpopulation of countries and the shortage of living space, if it can be called a theory, as [you] well know has been widely preached by many conquerors and in the fullest aspect was expressed by [the] raving [of] Hitler. Under the cover of this "theory," he unleashed World War II. Calling the Germans to war,

Hitler reiterated that the German people . . . are crowded on the territory they occupy, that they must conquer—"Lebensraum." Pointing to the East, he asserted that the territory at least to the Urals must belong to the fascist masters, that it is needed . . . by the German people as "Lebensraum."

. . .

Given up-to-date weapons of annihilation, it is now particularly dangerous and, I would say, criminal to search for wealth through the extension of "Lebensraum."

In the Soviet Government's message of December 31, 1963,[*] we proposed that states should not violate existing frontiers, should not resort to forcible methods of solving territorial problems. War must not be a means of changing frontiers. Only in this condition can peace be safeguarded. The only acceptable way of revising frontiers is talks. Any other way, as a rule, leads to war.

This is the truth and not my discovery. It has been confirmed by history. In general, I lay no claims to the role of prophet solemnly uttering the truth, as some people do.

. . .

Mao Tse-tung hints that the Soviet Union is too big a country. They like to emphasize in Peking that the Czarist Government of Russia had acquired too many territories and included them within its boundaries. We do not want to defend Russian Czars. Like other Czars, they were plunderers, waged wars of aggression, and sought to seize other people's property and increase their possessions. But there must be one approach to all aggressors of the past, whether Russian Czars or Chinese Emperors.

The Russian Czars waged wars of aggrandizement. And what were the Chinese Emperors doing? They also waged wars of aggrandizement and plunder as the Russian Czars did. Chinese Emperors tried to conquer Korea, and they seized Mongolia, Tibet, and Sinkiang.

Let us take Sinkiang, for example. Have the Chinese been living there from time immemorial? The Sinkiang indigenous population differs sharply from the Chinese ethnically, linguistically, and in other

* Document 6.

respects. They are Uighur, Kazakh, Kirghiz, and other peoples. Chinese Emperors conquered them in the past and deprived them of their independence.

Thus, if one turns to history and recalls how states took shape, one will see that in all states, big and small, Czars engaged in plunder, the only difference being that the stronger aggressors grabbed more and the weaker ones grabbed less.

· · ·

What are we after? We want no war, we champion peace. But if we are attacked, we shall defend our borders with all means at our disposal. The frontiers of the Soviet Union are sacred and he who dares violate them will meet with a resolute rebuff from the peoples of the Soviet Union.

· · ·

The territory of the Soviet Union took shape as a result of historical processes. The October Revolution granted all peoples of Russia the right to self-determination, up to and including secession, and they used this right. Some peoples seceded from Russia, others voluntarily united to form the Union of Soviet Socialist Republics. The peoples of the Soviet Union do not want foreign lands, but they will allow nobody to encroach on their lands.

The Chinese state is also a multinational state. It also took shape as a result of historical processes. Chinese Emperors were in no less a degree robbers than the Russian Czars and accumulated big wealth by robbery. The independent Mongolian People's Republic was formed and is developing as a result of the national liberation struggle, while another part of the territory populated by Mongols forms part of the Chinese state.

The bulk of the Kazakh people live in the USSR, and most of the territory on which the Kazakh people live forms part of the Soviet Union. On this territory, the Kazakh people set up the Kazakh Soviet Socialist Republic. This is the sovereign state of the Kazakh people and, according to the Constitution, the Kazakh people have the right, if they wish to, to secede from the Soviet Union. Some of the Kazakhs and the territory they occupy form part of the Chinese state.

71

The Kirghiz Soviet Socialist Republic forms part of the Soviet Union and is the sovereign state of the Kirghiz people. Under the Constitution of the USSR, it also has the right to secede from the Soviet Union if the Kirghiz people wish this. Some of the Kirghiz and the territory they occupy form part of China.

Territorial and national questions in the land of the Soviets have been settled in conformity with the expression of the will of the peoples. We speak only for ourselves and are not going to interfere in the affairs of other states. In other words, issues arising between states with regard to frontiers can be settled only on the basis of mutual agreement between these states.

And so we say: Let us not engage in incitement, let the peoples settle their destiny themselves. This is how disputes should be settled. One must respect the existing frontiers; we are in favor of self-determination of peoples.

27

THE SOVIET PROPOSAL TO THE UN ON THE PEACEFUL SETTLEMENT OF BORDER DISPUTES

(Excerpts from a dispatch from Tass International Service, Moscow, September 23, 1964.)

On September 22, acting permanent representative of the USSR at the United Nations in New York, P. D. Morozov, handed to UN Secretary-General U Thant a letter from the USSR Foreign Minister, A. A. Gromyko, with the following content.

DEAR MR. SECRETARY-GENERAL:

On behalf of the USSR Government, I hereby request the inclusion in the agenda of the Nineteenth Session of the UN General Assembly as a separate important question the item, "On the Renunciation by States of the Use of Force for Settling Territorial and Frontier Disputes."

Mankind's history abounds in sorry examples of how mutual or unilateral claims of states to another's territory grew into military conflicts and devastating wars, which cost the peoples so much. But weapons did not provide a solution to territorial disputes. They very soon again flared up with new force. Many territorial disputes were inherited by our generation, too. Moreover, these disputes and mutual claims have become even more numerous today.

. . .

Life shows that the majority of territorial disputes and claims over already stabilized frontiers of independent states are fraught with more than enough combustible material which might feed the flames of a great conflagration. Given the existence of ramified systems of military alliances, a clash occurring at some place directly between the conflicting parties would almost inevitably involve in such conflict tens of other states, including the Great Powers. Moreover, inasmuch as the armed forces of these powers are equipped with modern types of weapons, the entire depth of the danger involved in our time in what at first seem to be local conflicts will become apparent.

Having once started over unsatisfied territorial claims, such conflicts threaten to spread to vast areas of the world, even very remote from their flash point, and in the final run to grow into a world nuclear-missile war. There is only one way to avert such a fateful development: states must renounce the use of force for settling territorial and frontier disputes and recognize the principle that such problems may be solved only by peaceful means.

. . .

The considerations which prompted [the Soviet] Government to display initiative in advancing the proposal to conclude an international agreement on the renunciation by states of the use of force for solving territorial and frontier disputes are exhaustively clarified in the message addressed by the Chairman of the USSR Council of Ministers, Nikita Khrushchev, on December 31, 1963, to the heads of state and governments of the countries of the world.

It can be noted with satisfaction that the governments of most countries have positively received the initiative by the Soviet Government and expressed in their replies accord with the idea of renunciation by states of the use of force to solve territorial and frontier issues. This reinforces the hope that the task of ruling out of international life the use of force in international disputes between states can be solved successfully.

At the same time, the elimination of the threat of war conflicts due to territorial and frontier disputes would give the states an opportunity to devote more attention and effort to solving domestic problems, developing national economies, raising the people's welfare, and struggling against backwardness, poverty, and disease.

. . .

The United Nations cannot stand aloof from this important task, the realization of which would usher in a new stage in international relations.

The USSR Government expects that the Nineteenth Session of the General Assembly will pay special attention to the question of "Renunciation by States of the Use of Force for Settling Territorial and Frontier Disputes."

I hereby request, Mr. Secretary-General, that this letter be regarded as a memorandum, envisaged by Rule Twenty of the Procedural Rules of the General Assembly, and be circulated as an official UN document.*

[signed] A. GROMYKO
USSR Foreign Minister
September 21, 1964

28

RADIO MOSCOW TO ENGLAND

(Excerpts from a round-table discussion of Mao Tse-tung's talk with the Japanese Socialist delegation, a Radio Moscow broadcast to the United Kingdom, September 22, 1964.)

This past summer, Mao Tse-tung spoke to a delegation of Japanese socialists. He openly formulated Chinese territorial claims on the Soviet Union and went on to elaborate the so-called theory of repopulation of countries and shortage of living space. Premier Khrushchev criticized this theory and showed its danger.

. . .

It is no longer possible to use nuclear rocket weapons to attain

* This was done; however, as of February 1965 no action had been taken by the General Assembly because of the controversy over the voting rights of members (such as the USSR) who are delinquent with regard to peace-keeping assessments.

the aims sought by wars in the past. In the past, the aim was to smash the enemy's army, to occupy the territory of one or several countries, and to subordinate them to the victor's domination. None of these things can be attained with the help of nuclear rocket weapons. A nuclear bomb destroys everything—cities, factories, and the population—everything. Premier Khrushchev pointed out that the time is past when invaders could plunder the people with impunity and profit from war. Modern world war can bring no victory or riches to the one who starts it. The aggressor will suffer indescribable devastation and destruction. Starting a nuclear war is madness. Clearly, if the theory of expanding living space led to the destruction of Germany and Japan in Hitler's day and brought untold suffering to all the people, those who start a war today will meet with a much more staggering defeat and even complete destruction.

. . .

Communism aims at a higher standard of living, at a radiant future. That is why the Soviet Union rejects war as a means of settling international disputes, including those on territorial and border issues. No matter what problems arise, they should be settled peacefully, not by means of war.

29

STRONG WORDS FROM SINKIANG

(Excerpt from a speech by Saifudin, Chairman of the Sinkiang Uighur Autonomous Region, to a National Day rally in Urumchi, broadcast over Urumchi radio, October 1, 1964.)

Recently, Khrushchev himself made a personal appearance on the scene, clamoring hysterically and heaping venomous slander on Mao Tse-tung, the great leader of the Chinese Communist Party and the beloved leader of the people of all nationalities in China. Khrushchev, who has donned the mantle of Czarist Russia and collected the refuse abandoned by the imperialists, clamored that [the] Ili [region of Sinkiang] used to be Soviet territory and that Sinkiang does not belong to China.

But Sinkiang has always been part and parcel of the sacred and inalienable territory of our great fatherland, and its territorial integrity is to be protected as we protect our own lives. If the Khrushchev revisionists dare to stretch out their evil hands to invade and occupy our territory, they will certainly be repulsed by the people of various nationalities in Sinkiang and by the 650 million Chinese people. Their evil hands will be cut off as relentlessly as were those of the Indian reactionaries when they invaded China. The people of all nationalities in Sinkiang and the Chinese people throughout the entire country, who can boast of a high degree of awareness, are closely united and not easily intimidated.

30

THE CHAIRMAN OF THE CANADIAN COMMUNIST PARTY ON MAO'S EXPANSIONIST AMBITIONS

(Excerpt from Tim Buck, Chairman of the Canadian Communist Party, "Unity and the Need for a Conference of the Communist Parties," *World Marxist Review*, November 1964, pp. 11–16.)

The distinction between the vehement protestations of the Chinese leaders that they are dedicated to Marxism-Leninism and what they are really doing, found vivid expression in statements made by Mao Tse-tung in the course of an interview with a group of Japanese socialists.

Mao Tse-tung indicated to the Japanese socialists that he and his associates in the leadership of the Party and the government of China envisage the pursuit of aims and a state policy of which cultivation of prejudice and hostility against the Soviet Union is an essential part. In addition to describing the far-reaching territorial objectives of that policy, he suggested that Japan could well be a partner in the pursuit of its aims. "Japan and China should act in concert and cooperate with each other," he told the Japanese delegation. He even referred to some Far Eastern maritime areas of the Soviet Union which Japanese imperialism tried to seize following the Great October Revolution, as land which "became Russian territory" only "about a hundred years ago." He concluded his remarks with the words: "As for the Kurile Islands, the matter is clear. They should be returned to Japan."

The above deals with only one aspect of Mao Tse-tung's wide-ranging suggestions concerning possible territorial changes extending across Central Europe. His statements to the Japanese socialists had nothing in common with Marxism-Leninism; they were an expression of crude expansionist ambitions strikingly similar to those which brought widespread suffering and sorrow so often in the past.

It is impossible to ignore the fact that there is a direct relationship between the expansionist ambitions revealed to the Japanese socialists and the CCP leaders' efforts to split those Communist parties which refuse to support them. An international network of defenders of their nationalistic ambitions is a necessity to the Chinese leaders.